THROUGH A
CRACKED LENS

By

Marciana Ciresi

PURE GOLD! That's Marciana Ciresi's debut novel,
Through a Cracked Lens.

Julietta's family emigrates from Italy to Argentina shortly after World War II, when she is just fourteen. Her voice will delight and move you as you follow her struggle to find a new life there and turn her passion for photography into a career as a photojournalist.

The truths she uncovers in the process—about the war, about the governments involved in it and in its aftermath, about the human heart—will surprise you. Don't miss this unique coming-of-age story with heart-stopping parallels to our own time.

--Ann Harleman, award-winning author of Tell Me, Signora

CONTENTS

Acknowledgements

A writer in any genre benefits from curiosity, eager listening and reading skills developed throughout her life. Add to that mentors, teachers and storytellers and the writer becomes stoked by some revelation. So the journey begins. My interest in creating a story of an Italian family's emigration from Southern Italy to Argentina started with dinner at the home of my exchange student, Sol Blanc in 2004. Her parents, Roberto and Pati graciously hosted my daughter and I in Cordoba, Argentina at their home, inviting Roberto's father and mother who spoke no English. I conversed feebly in my Italian with them, learning they had left their beloved Italy after World War II to make a new life, free from Fascism. They were part of an exodus of many Italians, and other Europeans seeking community in a very Europeanized country which welcomed them with opportunities to grow businesses and thrive. But to leave behind your very heritage? I sought answers from that warm visit and knew this story was too big and relatively unknown to be left untold.

I visited Italy several times and returned to Cordoba and Buenos Aires, seeking familiarity with the places and people (see Walking the Streets in my newsletter) and finding first-hand material. I felt compelled to research not so much a scholarly treatise, but the history and stories of this immigration and I was shaken by evidence that the

Roman Catholic Church, the governments of Italy, Switzerland, Germany, Argentina, Uruguay, Brazil and Spain were complicit in providing safe passage to the elite Nazis who were perpetrators of the holocaust.

Encouragement and mentorship came from my treasured friend, Ann Harleman, herself an award-winning author, whose advice to join a writer's group and her commentaries stimulated me to create such memorable characters and events. On Whidbey Island, a writer's paradise, came Melinda Base, so helpful from the first day I recorded my story. Ana Kinkaid and Peter Schlagel the masterminds of Chart and Compass Creative offered greater insights and editing than ever I could have found without them. My close family, including Conner Gray whose readings and comments included tears, and my granddaughter, Kira who asked me to write a version for Scholastic, my son and daughter who listened to endless revisions over the ten years of research and writing, and Marianne Callahan who so loved the story she kept me moving forward. Thanks go to the talented team at Wordnality for their production assistance.

Researching the history often had me sobbing over the horrific consequences of Hitler's lust for supremacy of the pure Aryan race. Reading the novels of Mary Doria Russell, Kristen Beck, Mark Sullivan, Kristin Hannah, Jennifer Chiaverini, Alice Dujovne Ortiz and Ugo Goni, inspired me to be a better writer and tell the story with fierce truth. I believe readers will be as challenged and moved by its pathos and humanity as I was by my passion to write it.

PROLOGUE

THROUGH A CRACKED LENS

March 1947 Vietri sul Mare, Italy

JULIETTTA

"No, No, No. I won't go, Papa!" I screamed. I was furious. He confused me. I thought he loved me more than this!

"Nooo!" still echoed in my ears as I rushed out the kitchen door, leaving Mamma and Papa stunned. Huffing and crying, I ran up the hill, past lemon groves blooming their white stellar flowers. While sobbing, my nose dripped profusely, preventing me from smelling their usually overwhelming citrus fragrance. My Nonni would see their son, Carmine, was totally *testa pazza*! Crazy head! They'd let me stay with them if he proceeded with his plan.

"Julietta, calm the hell down and get back home!" my brother Nico shouted, chasing after me as instructed by Mamma and Papa, I was sure. I was winded but determined to rush away from what Papa wanted to be our new reality. Leaving this most beautiful village -- and the only home I had ever known, the only friends I had ever known, and my

Nonni! Nico was bigger and faster, but he didn't have the winds of fury at his back.

"Nico, get away from me! I'm fourteen and I get to decide my own life!" I wanted to stop to catch my breath, but I needed my grandparents now. "I'll stay with Nonno and Nonna until Papa comes to his senses. And if he insists on taking Zio Paolo's offer of a job and home in Argentina, I might stay with them forever until he sees how wrong it would be to take us away from our lives here, away from everything we love!"

"*Certo*! See if I give a damn whether you stay behind while the rest of us make a great new life in Cordoba. I love our home, but I see how the war has ruined everything about Italy, and Papa's war wounds and permanent scars keep him living in the past." Nico spoke as he broke stride alongside me and turned me towards him. "Juli, you come home and give Papa a chance to know what you feel -- besides your childish anger."

"I can't do it. I can't honor my father and mother as the Church teaches, because Papa won't respect me, and he's wrong, Nico! He's not thinking straight and I'm afraid he has talked himself into believing "for my family, Paolo's offer will provide a better life." I mockingly mimicked Papa's words while pulling away forcefully from my older brother. I just wanted to present my case and be listened to and consoled by my Nonni who would love to have me stay here with them.

This was the first time in my life I stubbornly resolved I would not comply. It might be a sin to rebel and refuse my Papa, but I saw clearly through my anger I would stay here forever. Of course!

Nico put his hand to my cheek to wipe away the tears, handed me the handkerchief he pulled from his pocket, and said, "Mamma needs you. She can't bear this either. She will be leaving her brother, Fabio, the only one of their family not killed by the goddamned Fascists. Be strong for her, Julietta. Come back and let her share your strength, not your anger."

"How can you be so agreeable to being yanked from your roots? I'm angry at you too, taking Papa's side! That makes it easier for him to push his plan on me and Mamma, and we hate it! I saw Mamma's shocked face, or didn't you even notice?" I asked him, bitterness in my voice matching the grim expression on my face.

"Leave Nonna out of this until Papa can tell her the news. Nonno is still at the butcher shop, and Nonna is probably taking her afternoon nap. Just come home, Julietta, " my brother demanded.

Sneering at him, I ran the rest of the way to my destination -- my Nonni's home, unchanged for as long as I have lived, and always my favorite destination. We have shared all the happy memories of growing up, and all the pains of war dominating and overshadowing our once peaceful life. The neighbor's hens, Rosa and Tessa clucked loudly, scattering to avoid my hurried entry into the garden leading to my Nonni's graceful entryway.

The noise startled Nonna, who was soaking her calloused feet in Nonno's side chair, between the smaller chair normally used by her, and the sofa which still appeared fresh and inviting after all these years. She grabbed the small, thin towel to dry her feet and called out to me, "What happened to you, bambina?" as I half fell into her arms. All the comfort I could ever ask for resided in Nonna's hugs and caresses and her sheltering embrace.

"Papa just insisted we will leave Vietri for a new life in Cordoba but I won't leave you, Nonna! Keep me here, please!" I was sobbing as these words spilled out and my brother abruptly entered through the open door. Nico began apologizing for my outburst and Nonna cut him off, sternly shaking a finger at him as she asked," Who has hurt my bambina?"

"Nonna, it's not like that. She's so upset she cannot be reasoned with!" Nico was cut off once again as Nonna told him to get to the point and make it quick! He continued, "Papa made an announcement about Paolo arranging for us to live in Cordoba. I think you should hear it from him. I'll go bring him and Mamma here. Julietta is really overreacting, just like she always did since she was a kid!"

Nonna motioned for me to sit on the sofa, wiped her feet dry, studied me and then Nico, and said to him, "Salvatore, watch out how you talk. Julietta is a delicate girl. She can't be forced into one of Paolo's schemes, which your Papa, in his condition, is too easily persuaded to agree to. Go now and bring my son and your Mamma here. Julietta stays."

Nico proceeded on his way to convince my parents to join us here, at Nonni's. Left alone with Nonna, I told her the story, beginning from the delivery that very afternoon of a telegram. It's a story I have held in my heart and has been the catalyst for my writing these last ten years.

NICO

Hoping to stay neutral and not appear as the bad guy here, I rushed back down the narrow spur off the road towards town, downhill to home. Just an hour ago, I had been sitting at our kitchen table, reading while Mamma was baking and the world was an everyday normal. Now I find myself caught between the Furies of three generations of women and the sweet lure of the Sirens captivating men.

I slowed down as I approached home, mentally re-living what had unexpectedly developed, beginning with Papa's arrival home an hour before dinnertime, holding a Western Union telegram. A piece of paper that would transform our future, if Julietta and Mamma could accept it.

I heard Papa from the kitchen arguing with Mamma. This was beyond unusual as they don't raise their voices even when I get reported for rude behavior. They don't shout at us to dominate and subdue us when Juli and I are stubborn, disrespectful or fighting as siblings will. They don't even argue loudly when they disagree. But it was getting heated as their voices clearly escalated to a level unimaginable to me. I tried to construct the possible arguing points which led to this impasse, but all I could come up with was Mamma was never going to agree to Papa taking us away from Vietri, and Papa was insisting he would make everything so much better for all of us by accepting Paolo's offer.

Hell, I was seventeen and mature enough to try to calm them both down with reasoning. I stepped through the threshhold into the thickest air as they shut down, glaring at each other and then at me. I must be a coward, I thought. I wanted to bolt back outside, but instead I stood in front of them, my heart pounding, my body shaking!

"Mamma, I'm sorry but Julietta is too shattered to leave Nonna. Please don't get mad, but I think you and Papa had better go there to explain to Nonna what happened and assure Julietta we won't be cut off from everyone here. She's not accepting any of it unless Mamma and Nonna reassure her. Papa, your mamma is upset and may have some questions to fire at you." I knew it sounded lame, but they quietly consented to go. Mamma grabbed a shawl from the hook near the door and hugged it around her thin shoulders, and we all trekked wordlessly to the home where Papa had grown up.

My papa, a resistance fighter who led thirty-seven men from our village into the Battle of Salerno to fight alongside the Allies in the fall of 1943, was my Nonni's last born and a favorite of his family. His courage was immense and proven in that fierce battle in which he nearly lost his leg during an assault he led, greatly outnumbered by Nazi Germans who had been fighting the Allied assault alongside Italian Fascists. Papa, like most of the villagers, despised both Nazis and Fascism which had taken possession of Italy under Mussolini.

Yet I detected some timidity as he approached Nonna, removing his cap and bowing his head. I'm also certain I saw a glimmer of sympathy wash over Papa's face as he looked over at his 14-year-old daughter's sad and tremulous face, turned now to him.

Focusing on Papa, Nonna spoke. "Carmine, you have a lot of explaining to do. You can start when your papa gets home soon. Meanwhile help yourself to wine and formaggio and sit over there, next to Nonno's seat, still warm from me sitting there, before my troubled bambina rushed in here. Angelina sit next to Julietta and me. I set some lemon water and cookies out for you. Nico, go meet Nonno and hasten him home, will you?"

I nodded and gladly departed as instructed. This was not the indulgent old Nonna I was always comfortable around. Was she or Nonno aware of the content of that telegram? I ran downhill, this time to Migliore's Macelleria, where I would meet my Nonno who had built this butcher shop with help from his papa and older cousins the year before he married Nonna. The Macelleria was the pride of our family and our village; I loved helping out every weekend, starting after classes on Friday, when we featured fish, as required by the church, and the entire day Saturday. Sundays all shops in Vietri sul Mare were closed, another requirement of the Catholic church.

My Nonno was sweeping the last of the sawdust from the floor onto the dustbin, so I offered to empty it, adding, "Nonno, we should hasten home where Papa, Mamma, Julietta and Nonna are waiting for us. We have received news that has everyone upset and excited, but I don't want to go too deeply into it until you are there to weigh in."

"It's not so often these days that I get the recognition I deserve of my status as patriarch of the family. Must be serious?" Nonno winked as he said that. "Nico, I was sure that something big was happening. It's pretty strange for a telegram to arrive for your papa and then have him push aside the flank steaks he had been trimming, toss his bloody apron into the basket, and rush out, hands still dripping after quickly washing them. I watched him rush out, grasping that telegram and whistling, so I wasn't worried he'd received bad news."

"He didn't tell you who it was from, or anything? Papa could barely contain himself as he called us to gather in the kitchen and read it. But that's all I'm going to tell you, to encourage you to hurry home with me -- to your house, of course." I directed Nonno to the darkening thunderclouds building directly over us and waved him on, as wind picked up, mirroring the stormy scene I was sure was awaiting our arrival.

NONNO

I may have raised three sons and three daughters, but not one gives me credit for figuring out what is happening right under my nose! I just let them assume I am oblivious so they will reveal, in their own words and time, complete details of events in their lives. Nine years ago, my oldest son, Paolo, began tiptoeing around, so even his wife Tina came, and asked if I had any idea what he was up to. With a few disclosures from her and my brother Giorgio, I only acted surprised when Paolo approached me about his imminent plans to emigrate to Argentina. Not so peculiar, dreading the increasing oppression and aggression under Mussolini and the Fascist Black Shirts, my oldest son could hardly wait to leave our war threatened Italia.

"Nico, slow down for your nonno! Let me catch up. You are like mio fratello, Giorgio, at your age -- only two speeds -- on your culo reading or one and a half the speed of anybody else! You even look like he did at your age. I'm telling you, he was also very smart, like you. Once the laws of anti-semitism were enacted in July 1925, Giorgio took his wife Judith Anna and their grown children to Argentina. He knew Mussolini's actual intention was to deprive our own citizens of their rights, training his black-shirted goons to carry out his increasingly tyrannical dictates. None of us Migliores trusted that lying bastard except my son Pietro who fought in his artillery and is still missing." Nico slowed down to hear more of what we rarely spoke.

"Nonno, your brother Giorgio and his wife were married in Vietri's cathedral -- you have their wedding picture in the Macelleria. So why did they rush to leave Italy when the laws against the Jews were set down?"

"My sister-in-law was an Italian Jew who converted to Catholicism to marry Giorgio. Her parents and entire family were quite dismayed, but all attended the wedding and baptisms of their four children. Giorgio was hired by the owner of a meat-packing factory in Buenos Aires, impressing them with his Italian skills butchering and packing la carne, and rising quickly to a management position. He earned great sums of money and brought Judith Anna's parents and family to Italia-friendly Argentina. Next, as you know, Giorgio wrote to Paolo and asked him what he was waiting for, Il Duce to declare war and they would lose everything? And you know the rest of the story, no?" I looked deeply at Nico who I felt was hiding something he wasn't telling me.

As the rain pelted us fast and hard, we ran faster and faster and reached home soaking wet.

MAMMA

Everything I cling to gets taken away from me. Fabio and I had taken the train from Bologna in 1925 to say our good-byes to our southern cousins, Giorgio Migliore and his family before they departed for Argentina to escape the anti-semitic laws that could have imprisoned them, even though Judith renounced her Jewish faith to marry Giorgio. They were our distant cousins, but Fabio and I loved any chance we were offered to take the train from Bologna for a holiday in the more rural, quiet village of Vietri sul Mare. We lost far more on that trip than our departing cousins. While we were away, our entire family was blown up and burned beyond recognition at our home in Bologna. We were told they were targeted by the Fascisti who suspected my father, a distinguished professor of linguistics at the University of Bologna, of harboring students who were subversive communist instigators. Without proof, they destroyed everything I held dear in the world, including my dreams for a future in which I would graduate from that same university. Grieving with my brother, I was sure I could never make sense of my life, and in that void, Rosario and Rosa Migliore rushed in with loving arms to embrace me and Fabio, and offer their home to be our home. I accepted. I was saved, and as I reconstructed my life within their loving safety, I also fell in love with their son, Carmine.

Grief struck again during the war; those countless times witnessing a constant stream of soldiers, near death, presenting atrocious gaping wounds, in the field hospital where I frequently assisted the medical staff. Death and gruesome hideous war injuries which could only lead to death, and the appalling smells, infections, groans and hysteria followed every battle. No guarantees of sterility, and inadequate supplies further plagued our medical outposts until we all felt we would lose our minds! And in the midst of that, I was one of a dozen volunteers to contract typhus. The graves of my prematurely miscarried twins resulting from that typhus bout will always remind me of the personal toll serving our resistance soldiers dealt me. I will never forgive Benito " il Duce" Mussolini!

Carmine would never have served under Mussolini! Childhood polio left him with a significant limp, keeping him from being conscripted and allowing him to stay in Vietri sul Mare working at the family butcher shop. While there, he gathered into a resistance cell, whoever amongst village men and women were known to be as anti-fascist as he and I. We couldn't liberate our Italy without help of the Allies, but our acts of daring gave our countrymen courage to become a fighting unit as part of la resistenza! His battle injuries nearly took him from me, but thankfully I only had to share our grief over his one serious wound, his nearly shattered leg.

I realize I should not consider this departure something to grieve. Only now, after all we have lived through, life here is yet another thing I had hoped to cling onto, and now is being taken from me. Holy Mother of God, I pray you once again help me endure. And please do not let my children suffer, I beg of you!

PAPA

Defeat, defeat, defeat.

This time my family is going to come out of difficult times a clear winner. My generation consists of adherents of Fascism, under the yoke of Mussolini's lies, and the majority of ordinary poor of Italy who willingly accepted the fallacy a strong leader equates to a strong country. We thought Il Duce would be leader over a great modern Italy. His craftily designed myth put our beautiful country into jeopardy as he led us into war in Ethiopia, depleting the army and our resources. That was the condition under which he led the fighting forces into Hitler's war. Duce's son-in-law followed his orders to go to Berlin and sign the goddamned Pact of Steel, both believing in 1940 the Fuhrer was speaking truth when he gave assurance he would not lead Italy into war for at least five years to give our country a chance to replenish its battered and depleted fighting forces and military equipment. Merda!

Official records I read in Life Magazine reported our military dead and missing from 1940 to 1945 were nearly 300,000, including over 17,000 resistance fighters. After the armistice with the Allies, about 650,000 Italian armed forces who refused to side with occupying Germans were interned in concentration camps. Imprisonment in those filthy labor camps killed 50,000. Civilian deaths after the armistice numbered over 150,000, and that doesn't count Italian Jews captured and sent to labor camps, nor Italian prisoners of war in Russia, some of whom, after barely surviving the harshest of conditions, died as they struggled to return to their loved ones here. Those mind-numbing numbers of my dead countrymen fueled my oath I would fight and would not accept defeat.

Then there's Fascism itself. The Duce rode that slick train into his position as party leader, as our cowardly King Vittorio Emmanuelle capitulated to the force of Black Shirted Fascisti to put Benito Mussolini into the top position of their Fascist government. Benito wasted no time forging a dictatorship over a movement aimed at war, territorial expansion and empire. All able-bodied men were forcibly conscripted into his army, many were sent to win back our mythical former Roman territories in Ethiopia and Libya, and more were sent to fight Franco's civil war in Spain. Meanwhile all businesses and institutions and the entire population of Italy had their liberties stripped away as they were forced to march in step to aggressive, hostile policies of a militaristic despotism. The Migliores did not! We suffered loss of our freedoms and deprivations of living essentials, but we never supported il Duce or his flagship Fascism. It was not about honor as much as about principles, but there would only have been heavy repercussions to anyone who openly protested beliefs they tried to shove down our throats. Sly and watchful, we survived and remained an unseen but important foundation for our village.

I can never feel attached to Italy again. Vietri will always have my heart as it holds my parents and friends who fought with me resisting the total evil of Fascism and Nazism. As we celebrated our wins, so we shall celebrate moving on, moving up, and in my case, moving away. All for a better life, and I don't see it happening here. There will be no Nuremburg Trials for Italy's murderous Fascists. In fact, many of them are in esteemed positions in national and regional governments as though they have been blameless these many years!

I'm sure I can convince Angelina, Nico and Julietta. Maybe even today...or soon.

ONE

THE TELEGRAM JULIETTA

*N*ico is on his way to convince my parents to join us here, at Nonni's because I am not going back home until Papa's visions of a grand new life thousands of miles across the sea are shot through with the reality his parents and wife and daughter and just about everyone else but Paolo wants us to stay here and make our lives here sweet again.

I am Julietta Migliore, a photojournalist whose life appeared to be heading for disaster, and I'm certain in some ways it nearly was. Photojournalists know indelible memories persist nearly picture perfect, unwaveringly complete when they are recalled. The fact we had never before in my fourteen years received a Western Union telegram, surely made that evening in the spring of 1947 one of those. My story follows the blow-by-blow account of events that propelled me to Nonna and Nonno's, as I told them from my troubled heart once Nonno and Nico arrived from the butcher shop, wet from suddenly pounding rain and slightly shaken from lightning and thunder. Looking back, may I have assumed that was what made them appear shaken?

Papa had left the butcher shop early, and with pain stabbing from his heel to the hip of his damaged left leg, rushed along the narrow winding streets of Vietri sul Mare to our home. He called out, "Julietta, join us, quickly," so from our herb garden, I dashed in to see him holding a yellow paper folded neatly in his hand. Breathing heavily, he gathered Mamma, my brother Nico and I together at the kitchen table, where Nico had been reading All Quiet on the Western Front. The lemon and *frangiapane* almond fragrance of Mamma's pear tarte, just removed from the oven, filled the kitchen that warm March day.

I shook some dirt from my skirt and knees, hoping the distraction of a telegram would keep Mamma from giving me the disapproving eye. The three of us kept hush waiting for Papa to read the telegram he grasped in his hand. Families with relatives in the military, fighting on battle fronts from Libya and Ethiopia to Albania and Yugoslavia, would dread receiving a Western Union telegram. If their soldier was an officer, an Italian officer would personally visit to notify your family of his death or missing in action status. Otherwise, that yellow telegram alone might inform that your missing soldier might never return, or was killed in action. In our town, the telegraph office was still delivering notices of that sort, nearly two years after war was officially ended in 1945. Mamma poured last season's cherry wine into the shallow crystal wine glass Papa preferred, before he read aloud the telegram wired by his brother Paolo, from Argentina.

MY COMPANY IS HIRING EXPERIENCED MEAT CUTTERS STOP YOU ARE MY FIRST CHOICE STOP GET HERE ON 4 SEPTEMBER SAILING OF M.S. VULCANIA FROM GENOA STOP TICKETS FOR FAMILY TO FOLLOW WITH ADVANCE FOR TRAVEL AND FIRST MONTH SALARY STOP YOU ARE HIRED STOP TELL LINA WE FOUND YOU A HOME

"My brother Paolo is ten years older than I am and I love him still looking after me!" declared my Papa, smiling broadly, while the rest of us could not even hide our disbelief. "Our family's proud tradition of being the region's best butchers is justified. When Giorgio and Paolo left and my brother Pietro was conscripted, it was Migliore's Macelleria, consisting of Nonno, me and the grandchildren, who continued to provide our village shops and people whatever meats and vegetables could be procured." We were familiar with this prologue and hoped he wouldn't need to mention again the childhood polio affecting his left leg, now shorter than his right, leaving him with a limp and unable to be drafted.

I couldn't contain myself, so I spoke out, "We all felt the loss when Giorgio's family left for Argentina. Then Giorgio enticed Paolo to emigrate as well. Paolo was gone only a year before he returned to pack his family up and whisk them off to Buenos Aires. They are enjoying their lives in Cordoba while our whole family and friends miss them, knowing it is far-fetched to expect their visits. The village has lost their contributions to the community, especially now everyone is trying to reconstruct what can never be recovered from Mussolini's war. And now, you want to take us away from our hometown, too?" My voice broke as I tossed out this accusation.

"Giorgio, Paolo, Argentina!" Mamma spoke rather sharply, while cutting pieces of crusty bread and salami for us to munch on. Digestion was another matter, but she continued, "They have a good life there, but I've never even considered leaving our country, and your leg is still in no condition to take on a move half-way around the world. Carmine, I'm so full of questions yet I feel speechless!" was all she could utter, followed by pulling her tattered but charmingly embroidered handkerchief from her apron pocket and dabbing at tears which welled over, liable to splash onto the floor. "Where did the money for this surprising generosity come from? What does he expect of us? How can we leave your parents, our home, and our butcher shop?"

In the warmth of our small kitchen with the counters and pantries he and his brothers had built for them as newlyweds nearly 20 years ago, Papa stroked the top of Mamma's head. "I have more than hinted I'd gladly join his thriving family in Argentina, so I'm only surprised after waiting this long, the time has come so suddenly." Papa then faced Nico and me and added, "Paolo was easily attracted to the prosperity of Argentina and its embracing of immigrants to work in its expanding industries. With her cities growing, each neighborhood required its own services." He paused long enough to enjoy a sip from the wine he held and sat down, continuing. "And with huge influxes of immigrants -- nearly 50% Italian -- my brother tells me new needs have opened even more opportunities. So, its cities are a welcoming place for workers making beer, pasta, and cheeses. We Italians are unquestionably the best in the construction, restaurant and meat industries! The United States has for years welcomed us to their shores for these purposes, and also because we are a very colorful people, no?"

Nico, rather than answering, jumped in, asking Papa about whether he might also get a job in Argentina's prospering economy. "I'll need to earn my way to the University my cousin Matteo is attending! But, ok, I'll shut up so you can speak your thoughts, Papa."

"Salvatore," Papa spoke, using my brother's formal given name. We knew a serious matter was to be presented when he called him by the christened name of my Mamma's deceased papa, instead of using his middle name, Nico. "Italian immigration since late 1800's has been Argentina's success story. In six short years since Zio Paolo moved his family to Argentina's second largest city, Cordoba, he has been promoted to assistant manager in the expanding meat cutting and packing industry and makes a very good living. As Paolo tells it, Argentina's economy is so productive European governments have been eager to purchase large quantities of their agricultural products, during the years of WWII and post-war. Europe could not have survived the war years without enormous shiploads of grains and meats from Argentina." How could we possibly be listening, while trying to deal with the shock of his pronouncement and imagine what it could mean for all of us.

Anger swept over me, feeling I was being ignored, and Mamma was clearly in pain. It wasn't fair! I had to find a way to be heard. I childishly screamed, "*Listen to me. I love my life here. HERE! I don't want to leave! Why doesn't it matter to anyone!*" That's when I bolted out to rush to the loving acceptance of my nonni.

Even now at age 24, I recall Papa's pronouncement the night he received the telegram, "Everybody knows there are no jobs, no money coming to us to rebuild these treasured cities and villages, roads and public structures. Nobody has savings to help keep their families fed, safe and cared for. The north of Italy will rebuild because that's where industry provides jobs and products. Southern Italians will not be able to modernize and will mourn for decades lives lost and lives shattered by Italy's participation in this war. Our memories will long hold regrets we ever held the belief Mussolini would provide a better economy. For this family, my brother's offer will provide a future and I will do everything in my ability to bring happiness and prosperity to our new life in Argentina."

Witnessing Mamma's expression, shock and tears, I tried to draw my own conclusion, but was instead left with tightness in my throat and a thud in the pit of my stomach.

Were we really departing, and would this be our final summer here!!

As she knew my feelings and could see right through me, Mamma softened her troubled expression, sighed and then smiled, leading me to the herb patch in the garden. She knelt down and patted the ground to invite me to do the same. As we resumed picking basil and oregano for dinner preparations, her hair coming undone from the bun she had carefully pinned into place before kissing Papa good-bye a short lifetime ago, she softly spoke for my benefit. "Julietta, *carissima*, to truly know the heart of the man you love, you must listen with more than your brain. Do you know what I mean?"

I shook my head with a faint "no" wanting Mamma to continue, sure she could clarify that reference and what significance it has now. She looked out to the horizon, seeming to smile within and continued, "You know you love someone when you will go wherever he goes. Papa finally can shed the misery he has carried since the Battle of Salerno, something I have prayed for, but I could not succeed in effecting. I want to share his hopes and dreams wherever they take us. Don't you see, Julietta, how much it matters to him we embrace his outlook for a new life in Argentina? If we also accept it as a promising experience in a thriving and beautiful country where his brother's family is eager to welcome us, we will share his happiness, and create our own."

I wanted to resist Papa's plans, and I felt it was impetuous and inconsiderate for him to persist. But in my mind, I began to accept departure as fact, although tears were again flowing, and my heart was breaking. I wiped my eyes, but turned back to see Mamma was also crying, then sobbing. She reached her arms around me, more to be consoled than to simply hug, so it felt natural for me to say, "I will always go wherever you go, Mamma. Following Papa seems more acceptable when I know you will keep me at your side and in your heart too."

Mamma put on a lighter face and said, " We've picked more herbs than we can use, so we should start dinner. I'll put on some Puccini to calm our minds. You and I can sweeten up the family discussion about our future as we indulge in the lemon gelato I made before these heated discussions might melt it, *si*?"

At that, I plucked an olive branch, walked back into our kitchen and handed it to my puzzled and disheartened father. "Let's be at peace, Papa, as we all grapple with what is possible and what just might not be acceptable." I was afraid if I uttered anything more, I'd become upset again, so I just moved close enough to hug him and receive his welcome embrace.

TWO

---●◆○◆●---

Sept 9, 1943
ARMISTICE, LIBERATION, FREEDOM?

Vietri Sul Mare shares its bay with adjacent Salerno, whose deep-port gulf made Salerno the targeted Allied beach landing for "Operation Avalanche." My guess is when they saw those precarious hill-town constructions, they feared firing on them might cause an avalanche! Most landings took place from Salerno south, even to ancient Paestum, where German snipers used ancient Greek towers to fire on the Anglo-American 5th Army. The Temple of Hera served as an Allied military tent hospital, and soldiers who gained the first beachhead in Italy used her sacred temples to hang their laundry and for other matters of personal hygiene, like shaving. The largest amphibian landing to date, the convoy consisted of seventy ships, 55,000 assault troops (with an equal number of reinforcements to follow), and inadequate supplies and munitions, which had been so hastily and carelessly packed that typewriters, file cabinets and white paint were easier for dismayed troops to find on the beaches than bombs and bullets.

Allied naval forces landed on the beachhead of the Gulf of Salerno on 9 September 1943, the day after the announcement of Italy's surrender. When they learned of their country switching sides from the Axis to the Allies, Italian soldiers surrendered to the Allies in joyous relief and huge numbers. Citizens exulted at the presumed arrival of peace. The Germans expected this move and were not caught unaware; THEY WERE READY! They dominated the critical defensive positions. Italian forces were quickly disarmed, and throughout Italy, many resistance fighters were forced to surrender and, on some occasions, murdered to the last man.

Here, the enemy held 275 strategic positions with machine gun nests, bridges and observation posts. ready to defend Salerno's beaches. Notably the Allies had not taken into account the Germans had set huge quantities of land mines in the bay, forcing the Allies to clumsily disembark men, machinery and supplies miles from the beach. And then there are the mountains ringing the gulf, from which the German Nazis could see and target all enemy movements. Finally, because Salerno was at the outer range of fighter air cover, the Allies could not provide more than meager air strikes which might have proved a deterrent to German superior position. Nine thousand Allied forces did not reach nearby Naples until 1 October. They would not enter Rome until 4 June 1944. Fierce fighting was the order of the day, each day until April's end in 1945.

Romero Gugliemmo saved Papa's life

The resistance fighters in our village had heard rumors the Allies, victorious in Sicily where they threw back the Germans, would land troops in the Bay of Salerno. Four of British General George Montgomery's 8th Army commandos landed at Vietri in the early hours of the morning on September 6, while Romero and three other resistance patriots were "patrolling" the beaches. At first, they were alarmed when they spotted the British commandos, as Italians were still part of the Axis, and as such were their enemy. The four resistance fighters remained in guarded positions, watching until they realized this could just be a reconnaissance mission. One of Romero's guards called out in his broken English, "What for are you here?" The English soldier called back, "Per liberare l'Europa dai nazisti!"

"Then let us help you liberate Europe from the Nazis," repeated our patrol guard using better English, signaling the others to approach these commandos and attempt to learn more. "We are patriots, anti-Fascisti è anti-Nazisti!" He called while approaching, as if they were already friends. "We know all what's on the beaches and our village, also Salerno."

The British commando who spoke Italian said their first task was surveillance, so assistance from the anti-Fascisti would be of great value. They were under orders to take out a German gun battery above the Vietri sul Mare beach. The Italian patriots pointed towards it and shrugged their shoulders. "It is without guards or defenses!"

The Italian-speaking soldier told his men to secure the town of Vietri, set up headquarters and open up the beach for Allied landings. He translated from our puzzled guard, who responded, "Salerno is where you will need to go up onto the shore. The Nazis are heavily in position there and you must take them out there to gain control of the pass from the beachhead to the road into Naples."

The two teams completed surveillance, and the commandos departed before sunrise to report back to British General Montgomery's headquarters in Sicily. At first sign of dawn, Romero and his "troops" were relieved of patrol duty, and returned home to sleep. In mid-afternoon, they met at an anti-Fascist coffee shop, sipped espressos and planned to gather other local anti-Fascists at sunset, on the beach. Romero then rushed to our butcher shop and directed their troop commander, my Papa to join. The resistance fighters from Vietri had several secret meetings with others from Salerno and its hill-towns over the next several hours, all agreeing to join the fighting sure to take place in Salerno. There was talk already Italians might break from the Axis to join forces with the Allies to liberate Europe.

Within days, the Allied landing at Salerno overwhelmed all the region's resources; the fighting was more fierce than imaginable! Medical personnel never seemed to take a break as soldiers were gunned down, mortar shells rained down on them, and new inexperienced troops from the United States were decimated. It was in the second week of fighting Papa's troops were pinned down by enemy tanks and machine gun fire. Witnessing several of his men wounded and killed, Papa rushed a machine gun nest, firing his automatic rifle. He stealthily advanced on the enemy, silencing the tank with a hand grenade, killing all occupants. He never knew what caused the explosion that nearly shattered his left leg before he passed out. Romero scooped my unconscious papa into his arms, tossed him on his back, and ran for the Salerno medical unit set up near the fighting. Papa woke shouting in pain, there being so little morphine available. Romero had carried him all the way on his back, stayed until the doctor told him Papa would live and could be healed, then rushed to Vietri to bring Mamma back to care for him.

Romero, soon after, brought Papa to Vietri's hospital by ambulance just days before the Allies claimed victory in Salerno and moved on towards Naples. He stayed on with resistance troops, having lost many under what then became his command. His objective became supplying ammunition, medical and food supplies to the fighters and those wounded battling for their lives. Needs were stupendous, and his big shoulders and great heart bore the weight and morale-boosting for so many!

One afternoon, nearly two years after the hellish battles had ended, while on our usual walks to help Papa regain full use of his leg, we were met by Romero, whose eyes glossed with tears as he remarked upon my Papa's progress. They embraced and Papa stepped aside so I could also greet him.

I sensed it was unlikely they would speak about their battlefield experiences with me present, but was certain there was much they needed to share. To give these friends some privacy, I pretended to chase after a rock I had kicked down the path. After several minutes, I returned to overhear fragments of their conversation.

Papa's voice was firm when he spoke to Romero, "Duce's ambition, the dreams to restore a Roman Empire in the Mediterranean-- their Mare Nostrum, nearly collapsed from Italian defeats in Greece and Africa. But villainous Mussolini had full German backing for his desire to turn the Mediterranean into the Roman empire it had been. He wanted to be Caesar!"

Papa winced in pain I still saw on our walks every day. He barely paused and added, "He talked about modernizing our country, while at the same time returning to the mentality of Roman Imperialism! The adulation of Benito, Il Duce, started with the image of Italy becoming great in our country's eyes and eyes of the world, *no*?"

Romero listened with serious concern and added, "The world after the first World War wanted no part of conflict. News leaked to isolationist countries from Italy and Germany became their own conceived image and propaganda."

Papa interrupted, "Both those Fascist dictators put in place the machinery to convince their populations of their vehement intentions to restore their countries to the greatness the victors of WWI stole from them. When you own the only permitted source of news, the people never learn the truth, only the propagandists' skillfully manipulated lies."

Romero nodded and added, "Il Duce proved not to be a ruthless, mind-piercing engineer intent on destroying human souls. The impression most of us had was he would create equilibrium, you know, a new status quo. Italians believed in him even as he grew Fascism to be the only party in Italy and he declared himself supreme leader."

Seeing my Papa slacken his pace even further, Romero slowed his more easy-going gait and took hold of Papa's upper arm. I knew they had shared pain many times prior — battlefield wounds to the body, psyche, spirit. Heartbreaking experiences I hoped I would never have to visit in my own life. But these men, wounded beyond life, redeemed their frailty by living with a gentle strength, their victories also shared.

"Carmine, the *Corriere* had flashed headlines and photos of Mussolini returning from Berlin, where he was courted by Hitler, the Grand Nazi! The truth is Mussolini was jealous of Hitler. Being outshone or out-militarized by a belligerent, like the German dictator, *non è possibile! Eh?* He forced on us peace-loving citizens his own program to toughen up the Italians. We watched him mobilize the power of racism with anti-Jewish policy, hold parades with troop formations performing the mandatory goose-step, and, above all, eliminate the bourgeoisie."

Papa paused in his walking to regain his strength, and said, "I have heard Duce saying, 'Incredible, the readiness of modern man to believe'. In a country so devout to Catholicism and family, no one was more contemptuous of the Italian character than Mussolini, with these very words, 'It is faith which moves mountains, because it gives the illusion that mountains move. Illusion is perhaps the only reality in life.' He mocked us, Romero, He mocked us!"

We waited a few minutes, while Papa composed himself, took the handkerchief from his rear pants pocket, as men always do to brush across their tear-moistened eyes, and blew his running nose. When he spoke, it was also for my benefit, as he turned to me and said, "Italy's part in the war is usually considered as one of failure and embarrassment because Italian forces were repeatedly rescued from defeat by their German allies. In terms of their motto 'Ferrea Mole, Ferreo Cuore,' Italian soldiers really had 'iron hearts,' though as the war went on, their too easily pierced 'iron hulls' increasingly let them down. Il Duce provided our troops sparse supplies, antiquated weapons and lots of bombastic lies."

Romero gripped Papa's hand, sharing his passion as you would with *amici più cari* and at the same time steadying his dearest friend as he concluded, "We shared the hope we felt when the King and Mussolini's replacement, General Badoglio made peace with the Allies. Hope when he switched sides. At Salerno, abandoning those earlier hopes, we resistance fighters were the patriots, fighting as one with the Allies. Under your leadership, Carmine, I would do it again!"

The three of us lingered, each filled with recollections of the crushing war and political atmosphere, for them surely charged with the overwhelming reality of death, horror, and hatred. For me, well, I was misery-struck by reliving the trauma, even while hanging on every word between them.

"*Mia figlia*, Julietta, Germans including an army of Nazi-sympathizing Italians fighting their fellow Italians dominated all of northern Italy but lucky breaks for the Allies and misguided Nazi leadership made our victory possible. You probably recall Romero railed on about that very subject on one of his visits, while I was still homebound."

I did recall a specific visit about six months after Papa's release from the hospital, in 1944. Romero was slicing salami he brought from our Macelleria where he had stopped to greet Nonno as he always did before his Wednesday afternoon visits to our home. Papa was sitting on the sofa, his damaged leg supported by extra pillows on the ottoman, his smile conveying he was very glad for the visit. I brought a basket of fresh crusty bread, some olive oil for dipping, and a pitcher of cold water.

"Angelina and Julietta, you must be taking excellent care of my friend Carmine. Look at the color restored to his face and the gusto he is finally showing for our afternoon snack!" Romero nodded and smiled at Papa. "Your own papa, Rosario has the butcher shop looking very appealing, but we both agreed without you there, it's bland and heartless! See what you bring to us with your caring about everyone! We all rely on your smarts and your heart, Carmine! I heard some news today -- our king transferred most of his powers to his son, Umberto. So, the old coward has relinquished most of his power while retaining his title. The whole Badoglio government in southern Italy and their fighting forces remain loyal to the king. How is Hitler going to retaliate against him for ousting his underling Mussolini now?"

Papa visibly brightened as he bantered with Romero. He reached for the magazine he'd been reading and said, "Look at this recent Life Magazine showing Allied attacks on Monte Cassino and fierce German counterattacks. Then at Anzio, Germans took advantage of General Clark's insecure commander Lucas, who brilliantly had led a well-managed landing on Anzio's beachhead totally surprising the Nazis. Where did his courage go when he halted his troops, fearing the strength of Nazi reaction? Kesselring rapidly counter-attacked with several units re-deployed from Southern France, the Balkans and northern Italy. Lucas' delays on the beachhead, rather than moving his forces to forge ahead towards Rome, gave the Germans opportunity to fortify their position, providing them all the advantages."

Standing in the doorway, Monsignor Oliverio removed his hat as he asked if he could come in. "How wonderful to see Romero's visit has you so lively, Carmine! I overheard you speaking of the Allied failure to push from Anzio to save Rome. Let's not forget Allied aircraft launched a massive raid against the unoccupied monastery of Monte Cassino, totally destroying it while Germans hadn't even taken positions in it -- they were below. Afterwards the enemy found ruins of our ancient monastery to be perfect bunkers giving them offensive location needed to attack and subdue our side! Can you believe it?"

Nico entered at that moment, announcing Vesuvius had erupted, displacing thousands from nearby Naples and destroying nearly a hundred American aircraft. "It's total mayhem and devastation and rescuers are rushing in. They need supplies of everything -- water lines have burst, broken gas lines are causing fires, and they need all the help they can get. Has God forsaken Italy?"

Monsignor led all of us in supplication to our Holy Father who seemed to all but him to have turned away His face. But instead of Monsignor addressing Nico's question, he turned abruptly and focused on his own hands, still gripping his hat, and placed it back on his head, apologetically bidding farewell.

While recalling that visit in the spring of 1944, I was walking alongside Papa and Romero. Assuming my far-off look meant I was bored, Papa attempted to regain my attention. Looking at me, he commenced conversation about the two devils heading up Italy and Germany. "Julietta, in 1943, with war still raging in Russia, Hitler faced another difficulty. The Allies, having pushed the

Germans out of Africa, invaded Italy. Hadn't Italy chosen to form an "axis" with Germany to crush Bolshevik Communism?"

I responded that's what the nuns taught in 7th grade and Papa proceeded, "Instead, the Italians threw out Mussolini and switched sides, leaving German forces and Fascist Italian sympathizers fighting a bitter retreat up the peninsula. "

Romero pointed out. "In North Africa, Hitler showed the stubbornness that afflicted his command style. Two of his Generals, Kesselring and Rommel, offered him different options. Kesselring wanted to make a stand across the center of Italy. Rommel argued for retreating north and using mountains as a defensive line. He was correct in noting the Alps would provide much better defenses, leaving more troops free to fight in Russia."

"*Si*, Romero," Papa spoke. "After initial indecision, Hitler sided with Kesselring. He was known never to accept limits of what he could achieve, and so he tried to beat the Allies on both fronts, a decision that would cost his forces dearly. That was the year we received the Western Union telegram that Private Pietro Migliore was missing in action. I grasped my mamma tightly as Papa read her the wire and she collapsed. The strongest woman I ever knew collapsed in my arms, and I swore I would be the fighter in our family -- for the resistance! Hundreds of men like you from our village and Salerno proudly joined Italian Liberation Corps, and it was an honor to have led a division of 37 men, most of whom survived the Battle of Salerno. Few survived without injuries, and some with traumatic injuries, like my nearly shattered leg."

Romero spoke to us, "I think the new Republic, Italy, should be recognized as such, and freed from stigma of association with its Fascist past. We believed we had been liberated from Fascism, but we found ourselves on the threshold of more hardship and oppression. Those same conditions had ushered Fascism in!"

Romero visibly lightened up, put his hands on each side of Papa's downcast face and continued. "Carmine, I have always admired you, since our childhood years when everyone could see you were a bright learner and a clear-headed leader. You know, on the visits I made while you were laid up with your leg injuries, I observed you had books and magazines, so I knew I could rely on you for information on important events and their significance, as well as for photographs of Hollywood celebrities! We have shared so much over the years. I cannot bear the pain in my heart knowing you are really leaving."

Three of my friends waved cheerily and called out as they ran toward us on this path. I smiled and waved back. What did my face really speak? "*Buonasera* Ani and Lorena. *Come va*?" I managed, smiling wanly. "Let's catch up at the seawall after dinner. I finished my book report and want to have you read it before I turn it in, okay?"

"*Certo*, and I can show you the new shoes we're on our way to meet my mamma and buy. You probably saw them in Tonina's Tesori, our favorite shop -- they're black and white oxfords, my first new shoes! And I need them now I have bigger feet than my older sisters!" exclaimed a rushed and excited Lorena.

I pretended to share their enthusiasm. After all, they were unaware of the upswelling of uncertainties inside my head. Nothing would replace my fears of leaving, and memories of seeing Papa in pain as he strove to get stronger walking Vietri's familiar streets which led to the sea, the mountains, the churches and cemeteries where lay the remains of our neighbors and *las famiglia*, taken by the actions of our vain ex-leader Il Duce.

Through tear-swelled eyes I looked at the hills of our Mediterranean Eden, blue-green where forested, and fleshy peach of exposed soil, terra-cotta orange rooftops and multi-colored house facades -- those familiar houses, some with majolica and ceramic panels, left deep impressions on me as I choked on emotions, attempting to subdue the awkwardness such powerful realizations evoked. I sniffled and blinked to thwart my tears, once again.

I finally understood the desperation experienced by defeated Anti-Fascist Resistance Fighters when I heard Papa's parting comment, "Romero, throughout the war, Italy had reached beyond its capabilities and had been rescued by Hitler. Bah! These were not acts of kindness. The Germans wanted the Italians on their side, but Hitler and his generals did not trust us, contemptuously referring to us as Italian underdogs." Papa added some curses toward Nazis and Fascism and spat on the ground before looking up, as Romero spoke.

"Ultimately, Carmine while bitterness remains, very few Fascists were punished. Truth is, our new republic has more avowed Fascists than anti-Fascists in municipal and federal positions, especially in the courts! Just look where we are now."

Romero hugged Papa and took my hands into his large paws, shaking his head and trying to mouth the words

"Arrivederci" while choking on tears. He parted, entering the tavern.

Papa tugged my short-sleeved school uniform shirt, wordlessly turning us to our home-bound path, away from the old town center. Though still youthful, his anguished smile suggested less of the confident naivete I would have seen on this man before having known six years of war.

Has war done the same to my looks, and my outlook?

THREE

━━━◆─○─◆━━━

April 1947

CAMERA OBSCURA

Wind and rain suddenly pelted us, so we quickened our pace and wordlessly, I gestured for us to enter our historical landmark church, San Giovanni Batista. Following me, Papa removed his hat entering the sacristy of this beautiful sacred building. More than ever previously, I felt the presence of the Holy Trinity as my gaze found the 11th Century wooden crucifix near the altar, under a coffered gold ceiling. This ancient symbol of our beloved Lord's sacrifice, placed behind the 17th century marble altar also displayed an alabaster statue of Saint John the Baptist for whom the Chiesa is dedicated. I asked God to steady me, calm my racing mind and help me understand my emotions. In the sacristy entry to this beautiful church, I stood trembling.

Needing to express my personal misery, confusion, and outrage, I never felt I could be so bold before, until these words burst out from me. "Papa, when the armistice was declared, and the Nazis were forced out of our country, people everywhere cried, hugged and celebrated our Liberation. Cries could be heard from every street, 'Liberation, finalmente!' 'Liberation, finalmente!' Most everyone felt certain this was act one playing out in a new time of freedom and renewal, but I see your sorrow has never faded. Why couldn't you celebrate hopes for the future most others believed in? Your heartbreak has sustained the pain your family lives under."

Papa touched my hair tenderly, tugging it a bit as he said, "Because I seemed to know peace would be slow to arrive here. I don't live out of beliefs, which can be twisted and made to appear like the word of God, itself. No, I live out of my convictions and morals, further forged by my pain."

That set me to crying as I added, "I am so sad, Papa. We never deserved any of this!"

"*Bambina*," he replied cuddling my head against his side, tears falling again down his cheeks. "Liberation has left a devastating legacy of destruction as we try to flush away the venom that poisoned Europe, to let it slip into the past. As if that is even possible. *Bambina, bambina!*"

While it was too much for a fourteen-year-old to digest, I would mull over that conversation all year, better comprehending authoritarianism in 8th grade in Argentina. My life may have been shattered by war with its traumas and by our imminent departure, but unlike a vase, when dashed against a hard surface is shattered beyond repair, my spirit would prove more resilient than I had ever tested it.

Monsignor Oliverio entered the sacristy and rushed towards us, offering towels and solace. Clearly, he saw consternation in our faces and awkward dripping presence in the beautiful church nave. "You two are quite a sight -- here, take these and let's have a conversation, shall we?" The organist was rehearsing some unfamiliar tunes on the pipe organ, and I would instead have loved to just kneel and be uplifted by music filling the church.

Monsignor's stiff and domineering presence typically left me cold. It felt like he was offering token familiarity, which I sensed was nothing more than gathering our youth for some lesson or other unlike the parish priests who conveyed genuine interest, modeled by Christ, the "Good Shepherd".

We genuflected and approached the altar, entering a pew to "have a conversation." Monsignor smiled obligingly at me and then addressed Papa. "Carmine, how are you doing these days? Is your pain manageable? You're in our prayers daily, at our services and the sisters' novenas."

Papa nodded his head and offered cursory affirmative responses, hoping, I guessed he did not have to be probed about his injuries. "Monsignor, my family will be emigrating to Cordoba, Argentina in September. We'll be joining my brother Paolo and his family where we can make a new life. I'm not a light-hearted, jovial young man anymore; I'm not able to restore my spirit in this country. Period."

"What can we do for you, Carmine? Our life here becomes more lively and lovely every day, and we look after one another. How can we serve your family, so you don't feel you must depart? My heavens, I married you and Angelina right here before half the town. I've christened both of your children and had hoped to preside over their marriages when the time comes. This is difficult for me to imagine!"

"What a loss Vietri will have to endure. How will your family left behind get along without you? Your Papa, Rosario is getting on in years, and has been the butcher shop's sole proprietor through the war years when his other sons were serving in the war or had left Italy behind for South America. That's taken a toll on him, as well as the pain he and Rosa have endured since learning of your war injuries. They are so close to you and your children. You're certain leaving here is best for your whole family?"

Papa seemed astonished Monsignor was trying to keep him here rather than blessing him for his decision to move on with our lives. "So certain I had planned to ask you for prayers for our upcoming journey!" Papa spoke up, his lower jaw firm and his eyes fixed on Monsignor, not without some trepidation. "I have not said I will not be returning.

You may yet be the one to marry my children when that time comes. Meanwhile, I do not consider I'm turning my back on my family and my village. No, in fact I feel I am launching myself, Angelina and the children into a great new country, prosperity, opportunity and more!"

"In that case, Carmine, I will bless four St. Christopher medals, and stop by your home after Mass on Sunday with wine and gelato. I want to hear all your plans. If your departure in September is from Genoa, that is amazingly fortuitous as I will be meeting with a congregation of senior parish potentates. I'll be your driver!"

"Then we will await your visit on Sunday, Monsignor. The sisters save me issues of Life and Time magazines they've already viewed. I'd appreciate you bringing those along as well. *Arrivederci!"* Papa pushed himself out of the pew and genuflected to the golden cross of Our Savior before turning and leaving with me.

We left church during the height of the rainfall, so we were soaked by the time we arrived home. Mamma greeted us with towels and laughter as we sat down to warm mint tea. She had freshly baked crusty bread, and while slicing it into generous pieces, she suggested something to Papa, who was leaning in close to her near the stove. He tousled my hair as he walked past me, returning within moments with a present wrapped in butcher paper and tied with butcher string. Handing it to me, Papa, joined by Mamma, said this gift should help me overcome the sadness of leaving. "Our hope is for you to make permanent the images, memories and moments that will matter in days and years to come."

Papa drew on all he knew of me when he presented the gift of a camera — a complex and hugely expensive gift, meant of course to excite my interest in our upcoming departure, journey and life beyond. I couldn't have dreamed I would hold so great a gift, and I began imagining using this wondrous camera to create new images and to compose new meanings as we became an immigrant family in Argentina. I made a vow this Leica I held would provide me focus and purpose moving forward with our new lives. It might take years of dedicated study and experimentation, but I intended to master this tool to express what I wanted to show the world.

In my voracious devouring of magazines Papa collected from the nuns, English-language periodicals (including Time and The Atlantic), I admired Margaret Bourke-White, one of their star photographers and Gerda Taro, the first female photographer to cover a war zone. I could, and therefore would exchange my unwillingness to leave for a willingness to proceed with the life my Mamma and Papa were already anticipating. The opportunities this camera would create for me would start as soon as I could learn the operating techniques of loading film and adjusting lenses.

FOUR

***

May 1947

WHAT LIFE HAD BEEN

Reviewing my earlier life, I'm aware of a peculiar parallel reality in which Southern Italians like us led difficult lives from Mussolini's invasion of Ethiopia and generous 'involvement' in the Spanish Civil War, compounded by the scarcity of all goods during the war years. There was little but poverty, misery and despair throughout Italy and nearly all of Europe, we learned mostly from radio newscasts and beaten-down soldiers returning from battlefields. Factories throughout Italy, as in all of Europe, were modified and re-employed in the war industry, supplying everything from steel for ship building to canned food for the troops. Our village suffered rationing of petrol, food and anything factory produced. But my own family never went hungry, even while Papa was fighting with the Italian resistance once the Allies arrived in 1943. We had the Macelleria, our neighbors' hens provided eggs, and Nico and his friends would show up with fruits, olives and nuts picked from our Nonni's orchard and gardens when they helped with the harvest.

Nico at seventeen, was tall as Papa and nearly a foot taller than Mamma but had her rosy complexion, dark brown eyes and chestnut brown curly hair. His nose was angular and large like Papa's, while I was already Mamma's weight but half a foot taller and blessed with my Papa's straight auburn hair. My Papa's hazel brown eyes rarely sparkled as in pre-war days when I'd beseech them with my own. Only Nonna and I had truly green eyes, and I believe that may have been why I was her favorite.

She and Mamma were teaching me to cook and to paint ceramics in the style my village was so celebrated for. Vietri Sul Mare in the province of Salerno, considered the first pearl on a string of beautiful villages and cities along the Amalfi Coast, is known worldwide for its ceramics, whose production dates back to the 1600's. Its enamels and decorations contain all the colors of the Amalfi coast: deep blue of the sea, bright green of the Mediterranean vegetation and golden orange and yellow of its citrus fruit. In the terraced alleys of the city's picturesque and historic "*centro storico*" time moves at a slower pace. Townsfolk know and greet each other; they walk through alleys and archways happy to encounter their *compadres* and stop for a chat. Clotheslines are tied between your own window and your neighbor's across the alley, fragrant basil is grown in pots in front of often open doors. Small statues of Virgin Mary are lovingly decorated and adorned with flowers, and children are quite naturally picked up from school by their *nonno*, grandfather or *nonna*, grandmother. Here, amid local everyday life visitors are sure to gain insight into the soul of "Bella Italia."

Food and family always accompany memories of our village life in Vietri. Nonna picked greens like cardoons that grew wild around our town, especially along the humble walk over the small hill past the lesser church of Santa Margherita. On her visits to us, she carried two or three mesh bags containing greens, a pie, sheep's cheese and sometimes eggs from her poor cottage neighbor. I was always thrilled to greet her and help wash and remove the tough strings, pulling them along from partially trimmed bottoms, as with celery. She would boil the greens, dry and dredge them in flour with salt and pepper and fry them in olive oil, adding beaten eggs once lightly browned. Her frittatas were divine, accompanied by papa's browned sausage and Mamma's crusty bread spread with fresh cream butter.

In pre-war times, roasts of lamb and Cinghiale (wild boar) were served at holidays, but we always had sweets! My mouth waters as I recall the Sfinge di San Giuseppe, those fried sweet dough balls filled with custard or ricotta cheese and a little orange peel. We made towers of sesame seed anise cookies we called giuggiulena and chocolate spice cookies, orange frosted rounded cookies and of course, thumbprint cookies rolled in ground walnuts, their indents filled with homemade preserves. For weddings we made many, many cannoli and for Christmas we spent days making cuccidati, the fig, date and walnut stuffed cookies infused with some whisky, and when frosted, sprinkled with green and red sugar sparkles. Always present were Nona's pizzelles, anise or lemon flavored, made in an ornamental round waffle iron and dusted with powdered sugar.

Sadly, years after 1940 demanded the victims of Fascism and Nazism provide our bounty to their forces, so our traditionally prepared *cenas de famiglia* were diminished by what little we could procure on our infrequent visits to neighboring Salerno or Napoli. I lived the first eight years of my life in bliss, but later in terror until on May 25, 1945 Germany signed an unconditional surrender, spreading celebration across Europe and the U.S.A. as the Allies declared victory. European liberation began but recovery was slow and continued years after Papa read that telegram from Zio Paolo to us in the spring of 1947.

I knew Papa was depressed. Nico confided it seemed Papa went through the motions of resuming life in Vietri. Recovering is depressing, but not dismal. War memories coupled with the recovery period – these are dismal. The price of Il Duce's power has been misery and death; the cost of his tyranny has been the loss of our liberties.

Every patriot fought for his individual freedoms, right to life, and especially for restoration of liberties lost as a result of naked Fascist aggression and the Nazi's unprovoked war. Papa with the heart of a fighter summarized his plight, while still on a cot in the medic outpost, "Mussolini drove us into war with the lie, with love if possible, and with force if necessary. I wanted to believe that message, Julietta, because that is my truth. Contrast that to the motto of the Blackshirts, *Me ne frego* or I don't give a damn."

My Papa was one of nearly 350,000 partisans and resistance fighters of disparate political ideologies who operated all over occupied Italy. German forces continued battling hard against the Italian anti-Fascist resistance until, following their defeat in the battle of Rome in 1944, the Germans eventually retreated out of Italy entirely, brutally destroying everything and executing anyone suspected of connection to *la resistanza*. With nearly half the Italian soldiers taken prisoners and held in labor camps where many died, it took the emaciated survivors time to return to their families. Many had wives who had taken their factory jobs, and returning captive soldiers wanted them fired so they could have their jobs back. Plus the friction between those who supported Fascists and the partisans was not at all solved. There remained the vast undertaking of finding and dismantling Nazi and Fascist regimes throughout possibly the world! Now war victors would be faced with hunting down horrendous criminals and making them pay with their lives for the more than 50 million war casualties for which they were responsible.

The wind of change could hardly sweep in optimism considering those conditions, so who could wonder that our citizens wished to start anew. My family and our friends could hardly wait to cast off the oppressive weight of the terrors, scarcity, deaths and shattered futures to rebuild.

FIVE

FAREWELL TO ALL

The rains, visible in every direction from our hilltop walks dampened my spirits as my best friends and I walked to the soda shop three blocks from our school. In earlier years we might have skipped along or dashed, dodging raindrops. Now, I recalled my Nonna's yearly comment, "April, *omni goccia e un bacio*". Sure every raindrop is a kiss, yet just now, each helps to wash the tears down my cheeks. It's time to tell the girls the secret I can hardly keep, and so while exploding in tears, I say what I'd rehearsed.

"In five months I will be torn forever from this world of all my favorites!"

"Are you being threatened?" asked Ani, one of my two closest friends. What gave her that idea, I wondered? But then, she regularly felt intimidated since the war took her older brother and cousins away in their youth. Bitterness, misery and fear crept around us through the war years and became a habit you would recognize in heads no longer held high, faces looking dreary and weary.

"I've been worried your papa is going to need more medical care for his wounded leg than he can get here." Lorena spoke through tears. "But that can't take you away forever, unless the problem is maybe more mental. No! You can live with *la mia famiglia* forever! That's that!"

These responses tore at my heart as much as the pangs from my departure. We had never been separated. They would remain here, together, sharing teenage secrets and awkward moments of dating and maturing. All those upcoming life stages of romance and love pains, of marriages celebrated by young and old in the entire neighborhood. We always assumed we'd be sharing the raising of our babies, involvement in their school, and eventually the burying of our *genitori*, who had parented and grand-parented us! My teenage friends and I saw the future years as continuation of our present, and the generations preceding ours. Even poverty and hideous scars in the wake of six years of war would be put behind us as we struggled to recover, and we assumed we all would.

I continued, "Papa has taken a job in Cordoba, Argentina — in South America — where my Zio Paolo is a supervisor in the meat cutting and packing industry. Well, he's found us a home near his family in Cordoba and has wired tickets for our family to board an oceanliner leaving Genoa on 4 September."

Amidst tears and hugs smothering me in the rain, I sank again into thoughts of refusing to leave. How will I ever overcome these moments of misery? Will I return to visit often enough to remain best friends forever? Will I make friends close enough to fill these places in my heart?

I talked to Mamma about this. She held me and rocked me while we both sobbed, my head so near her head, my heart beating alongside her heart. I felt like we were one.

When I talk to Nico, he tells me I am obsessing because I am afraid. I fear the unknown. So common, he says. As if to reinforce his courage I saw him jut out his chin and say, "I am so ready to cast away all this poverty, this mind-sickness from past traumas and evidence of war."

"I am too!" I retorted. I felt I could never push aside memories of the terrors that shook the core of my being.

Nico lit a cigarette and offered me one. "Sis, I bet you will be smoking once we start making friends in Argentina.

Ha! I think I saw your friend Lorena smoking with her cousin last week near the church's thrift shop. You sure you don't want a drag?"

"Nico, you won't find me engulfing my body and clothing with those nasty cigarettes! Have you offered any to Mamma? No, but you think I should begin a habit so distasteful? Save your breath, and, while you're at it, don't breathe on me!" At which, I waved smoke away with my hand and Nico blew smoke rings above his head, uttering off-handedly, "If these land on my head, they'll place on me the only halo I'll ever have!"

I continued where I left off, "It was frightening to have Papa fighting the battles at Salerno, the violent source of bombs, smoke and frequent truckloads of soldiers and local people with varying degrees of bloody traumas." I had to wonder, was I a timid coward?

Nico kept right on, "I despise Mussolini and *Fascismo!* My friends and I cheered when we heard that bastard had been shot in Milan, by partisans who recognized him on his flight to Lake Como. They executed him, and the mobs hung him upside down, in Milan's main square on the same spot anti-Fascists had been murdered! So died the founder of Fascism – *Il Duce* – shot in the back as befits a traitor! I wanted to fight with the resistance alongside Papa. If Nonno had not so quickly realized Donnie and I had snuck out to assist our fighters being bombed and overpowered at Salerno, we would have fought those bastards with all our might! American Rangers and paratroopers landed there and all around the area under heavy bombardment. The Americans who landed on the beaches in early September, almost retreated, but instead kept pushing nearly to Naples.

That damn German fighting machine had to back away as Allied forces took control of Naples."

"Nico, you're only adding to my fear. Mine is of the unknown; yours is of the known. And quit using so many cuss words. Your excuse all soldiers behind the lines cuss is a lie! Papa does not!"

"Juli, your sentiments are so childish. When we heard the shelling, saw flames and smoke blackening the sky from the air and land battles, and the fear on everyone's face, that was only a small dose of the unthinkable horrors out on the fields. You bet there was goddamned cussing!"

I nearly wailed, "Nico, in my fear which you consider so childish, I prayed every day, often saying the rosary with Mamma and Nonna."

"Juli, Juli," my brother continued, his voice softening. "While we offered prayers our men would endure and return whole and victorious, we knew they were dying with every German assault. We're still living in crisis and misery. So, keep up the prayers!"

Without missing a beat, Nico related a battlefield incident he witnessed before being forced back to our home by Nonno. "Donni and I watched as a private barely twenty years old zig-zagged into intense enemy fire, entering a heavily shelled building inside which were a troop of German soldiers. Our fighters couldn't move into that barrage, but also couldn't stay in their vulnerable position. So, this soldier entered the building, forcing out the German soldiers. Setting out again severely wounded, he dashed across the 20 meters toward the main objective, taking that building. He fell as his unit surged around him to victory. This type of 'win,' at huge expense, was repeated by troops throughout our country. And still the Germans pounded us. Sometimes we would surrender ground; often we were forced back." He drew deeply on the cigarette, then stubbed it out and turned to face me.

Seeing me in tears, he concluded, "The losses were overwhelmingly huge. The fighting could not have been more intense. The needs were, and still are, never-ending. And victory has left us with war-spoiled land, water, buildings, hospitals, schools, churches, orphaned children, and families everywhere devastated from deaths and injuries. I regret I wasn't allowed to join Papa when the fighting came within earshot of our own town. At least my classmates and I are now rebuilding the torn-up roads and bridges, restoring fields and farmlands. Oh, I will fight, against lies, injustice, oppression and Fascism, if I see them in our new homeland of Argentina!"

Nico's anguish is usually subdued. Perhaps it is his alternative to tears. Perhaps my own anguish is meager compared to my brother and my Papa, but I still have five months to put all that aside and keep my chin up. Will we carry this anguish throughout our lives? Will it reside in our genes?

And what of our mental horizons and pierced souls -- throughout our lives?

SIX

⸺●○●⸺

April 1947

FINAL FOCUS

F inally revealing my secret to my best friends, Ani and Lorena, it is a done deed. I lied to them surely we would be back, knowing after family discussions it was apparent there would be no desire on Papa's part to return. He shared with me his heart has been broken continuing to see everywhere the abysmal poverty, poor veterans' care, and emigration of many Italian families like ours to the Americas. Staying here would remind him every day of the horrors he witnessed and misery millions faced -- and probably would never recover from.

I told the girls Papa cannot live in the paralysis of these conditions, and they should share my buona fortuna -- I could live in a modern country with plenty of food, great culture, and a river that runs from my home all the way into town. Argentina even has a beautiful First Lady! I showed them glossy photographs which I had cut from Life, when Argentina's President Juan Perón's wife, Evita, made a glorious sweep through Europe, promising bountiful food and meat (in exchange for what, I wondered?). The gloom lessened on their pretty faces as they began to see my hope while I revealed my future and my dreams. Before we began to dwell too long on the departure, I begged them to help me memorize my part in the upcoming May Day procession to the Immaculate Mother of God. Called the Magnificada, it is the song of Mary, which begins "My soul magnifies the Lord".

"Next month I must be prepared for the important role of young, innocent Mary, as I'll be speaking the Virgin's response to Angel Gabriel when he announced to her she'd been chosen to be *la Madre de Dio*.

"Oh that!" Ani said. "My sister played that part last year so I helped with her lines, just like I'll help you. She was so nervous she tripped Michaela, who played Gabriel, when he reached across to her with his hand out in a blessing."

"We couldn't help but laugh when her overly long head scarf got tangled in his overly long slippers!" Ani's memory lightened the rest of our walk. We resumed being a best friend trio as we reached the soda shop and ordered lemon ices.

As a child I wasn't able to memorize anything not set to music or using musical cadence. Naturally I would experience stage fright if I had to participate in school plays requiring speaking lines. But I adored pageantry played out in religious and civic events, in life's landmarks, nature and art. I was told I had the vision of an artist, capturing details, composition and the hidden. I tracked every bird's activity and sound, sighting them easily when others never noticed them. Even my closest friends usually saw only what I pointed out directly.

"Lorena," I spoke quietly to her one day last summer, "follow that trill and twitching branches as the seasonally present bird couple, the *rondini* alights and hops along to their favorite hiding place. Look — there!" I pointed twenty feet higher than where we stood, under the lemon tree already picked clean of its luscious fruits.

"Julietta, I see it! Show me more!"

Encouraged by her enthusiasm I walked her in utter quiet to a rock outcropping under an olive tree, pointing out spots of white and purple bird droppings, indications the parents had spent the past months constantly coming and going while raising their family.

I pointed up to their now abandoned, still intact nest. Eager to explore more, we moved the pickers' ladder to level ground just below the perfectly formed but nearly hidden oval weaving of twigs, feathers, grass and leaves. I let Lorena ascend to closely examine the nest.

"Please say I can take this down. There are fuzzy small feathers in it. Please!"

"Since the parent birds will build a new nest next spring, you can keep this one. I watched them build it and I've also seen orioles and bluebirds nesting all over our neighborhood." The sheer delight I experienced when seeing my friends enchanted as they discover what I uncover still motivates me. See, seek, examine, and create indelible, detailed impressions...I was a visual artist though not a graphic one. Nico would patiently instruct me to draw as he'd taught himself, by carefully reproducing on paper what the eye sees, using proportions, shapes and both bold and subtle strokes with a pencil. Nico's drawings recreated life, beauty, time. Mine were depictions — accurate but flat, devoid of the graceful intrigue present in art.

My flair seemed to better encompass scenes and lives. Mamma and Papa often mentioned the way I described these created "works of art", as the visuals I focused on and stayed in my memory, so like vivid pictures.

Here it is April, our last summer together before I would leave, and already I'm choking on memories and creating diversions to keep from descending into the dismal truth memories will be all I will have remaining. Really, my friends had suffered through these war years even more than I, losing family members and livelihoods, treasures and essentials. We shared everything, and cried over deaths and injuries of close family members and neighbors. We cried over my Papa's leg so torn up Mamma, Nonna, Nico and I took turns around the clock attending to his injuries. We comforted Papa when he shouted out in his nightmares any time of night, and we assisted him with painful exercises needed to regain use of his leg. I knew it was time to reveal their surprise gift, and to capture with it the first visual pictures of a day I would hold in my dearest memories.

"*O mio Dio!*" exclaimed Ani. This camera is amazing and perfect for you. Show me how to take a photograph and I will shoot one of you and Lorena, please!"

"Ok, I will focus it first at the correct distance, so you'll have to stand right here and make sure we're in the center of the view finder. That's the lens to which you will put your eye for the 'view', haha! Be certain to hold the camera very steady, then depress this button. The shutter will click so you'll know you have successfully taken the photo. I'll wind it to be ready for the next one I want to take of the two of you." I adjusted Lorena's straggly hair back into the barrette which barely performed its job, being yet another sister's hand-me-down. Then I returned to the task of setting the camera for a formal picture.

After a few clumsy attempts, Ani took our photos, but I didn't ask my friends to smile for my pictures of them. Nobody could revive themselves from the shock; there was little but sadness, little but desperation, little but dismal required preparedness. I wasn't sure it was the right thing, but sometimes I took photographs of misery we all hoped to forget, and sad defeat I saw in faces of people unaware they were subjects of my photos.

Pain is part of living which we cherish in the satisfaction from being freed. Well, I would be capturing smiles and tears in coming weeks of festivals, springtime weddings, final dinners and departure. Moving on requires something to build from, and I want to hold forever all my observations of this time.

I flew in the house to tell Mamma what just transpired between my best friends and me, feeling both despair and hope. It had been so clear, as friends and schoolmates, we'd always share our lives and interests. We just knew and loved each other too much not to share everything.

Mamma cupped my chin into her hands, lowering my eyes directly into hers, and began to laugh! "Julietta, your brother, Salvatore, was born predisposed to demand fairness. Never satisfied in the appearance of it, he would harangue whoever was the perpetrator of unequal justice until they gave up resisting him and re-distributed equally whatever Nico demanded. You, carissima were born with a heart for loving all things: living, imagined, created -- even rocks and dirt. If your compassion could be distributed throughout the earth, we'd be better for it, and there'd still be enough for the angels to press onto the avowed hard-hearted to ply them towards appreciation of God's gifts, great and small."

Somewhat uncomfortable with being complimented, I squirmed a bit and then put my arms around her. She seemed so small, while being so large to me.

"Julietta, I pray you live to a hundred years old, so you can continue to offer your pure heart and ability to commune with nature with all sorts of people. You have an extraordinary gift of empathy and kindness, which draws people to you and they willingly give you their trust. Like Saint Theresa, the Little Flower, *mia preciosa*, you draw out innocence often hidden behind masks imposed by an otherwise uncaring world."

"Oh, Mamma! I love you so deeply," I cried out to her. "Funny, how you can make me even love Nico while you are praising me up." I choked out my response as she held me, and we laughed together.

SEVEN

August 1947

FEAST OF MEMORIES

Nonno and Nonna gifted me with ten canisters of film, thirty-six exposures each, along with dozens of flash bulbs for my upcoming departure. Mamma's brother Fabio sold Papa's set of butchering knives and Nonna's beautiful Spanish mantilla to purchase the Leica camera and film. Zio Fabio added substantial cash to have photos made into prints to send back to my Nonni from Argentina. Holding these treasured and unfamiliar gifts I felt exhilarated for the future and less apprehensive about leaving this home. It was not abandonment if I could stay connected, at least with pictures, of our new adventures.

Embracing promises of a new life for my family away from the war-torn country my Papa no longer felt part of, I allowed myself to drift away from what I'd never pondered leaving. It would be like change itself is -- uncertain and exciting, offering opportunities while shutting doors. I was fourteen so I would have to be ready for it.

Naturally, I spoke to Mamma as she prepared manicotti crepes, while I mixed the ricotta with grated parmesan, chopped parsley and beaten eggs, testing for salt and pepper. "I sort of remember Christiana and Anna, my favorite cousins -- and they still are, you know. Do you think we'll become really close again when we join them in Cordoba? You're Christiana's godmother so it's your right to be close to her and guide her, just as Zio Fabio is to Nico, his godson."

Without burning her thumb, Mamma lifted the thin crepes from the small sizzling fry pan, sized perfectly for these discs we fill and bake with her *suco*, the savory, meat-laden, slow cooked tomato-based spaghetti sauce.

"*Certo*!" Mamma replied. "They write you with the same enthusiasm as you shared before they moved six years ago. Zia Tina said she'll take you to their school, swimming club and singing teacher. Oh, my God! Cordoba is going to be such an amazing place to live, and within a few blocks of them. I'm not sure what it will be like for me being a house mamma, but I intend on using my Red Cross nursing skills from years I volunteered caring for soldiers and civilians, casualties of war. I hope you take full advantage of the possibilities that come with living in a large city with colleges and universities, and so European! How lucky Zia Tina and your cousins are already embracing us!"

"Christiana is a year older than me and is preparing for high school. What if she has matured too much for me? Anna is nearly twelve. I know she'll hang out with me. Nico told me Christiana attracts many boys, Mamma. I'm going to snap a photograph of Nico's face when he's watching her but not aware of me. Keep that a secret between you and me, ok?"

Her chuckle told me Mamma agreed.

"Anyway, I'm tall and athletic like Christiana so she's saving some of her clothes for me. I don't want to stand out like a foreigner of no means. They'll need to teach me advanced Spanish so I can keep up with schoolwork. It'll be so hard to get used to the seasons being reversed!" I seemed to blurt out concerns eating at me whether or not they were relevant.

"Juli, you will learn and adapt fast, and I'm the one who will be so far behind. Here, add a spoonful more filling to each manicotti shell and stack them closer together. I have to prepare our dinner *insalata*."

I saw Mamma looking sideways at me to see if I appeared reflective or uncertain before she spoke again. "To me, some of the most beautiful words are: I learned, I am learning, I have learned. I will learn. A life of achievement is wrapped up in being able to say these words about your experiences."

Seeing me about to cry, she exclaimed, "*Abasta*! Finish up, set the table and tell your brother to walk your Nonni over here for dinner. Nonna has made cannoli! She traded some poultry from our butcher shop for pistachio nuts and sugar needed to sweeten the ricotta filling."

When my Nonni arrived, there was the usual hugging and busying of ourselves to prepare for the family dinner. Papa would be arriving soon, cleaned up of any evidence of today's butchering.

I had grown up seeing and smelling butchered and prepared meats, sawdust floors, bloodied aprons, and saber sharp knives. I'll never forget the joviality of Papa and his brothers, and my Nonno making this market the destination for Vietri's families and restaurant owners. Nico and I sometimes helped him wrap cut chops and ropes of sausages for customers or to be placed into the walk-in cooler. Our town newspaper had recently written a feature article with a photograph about Macelleria Migliore, making the family butcher shop even more famous! Behind the refrigerated display case with chops, sausages and internal organ meats lined up, prices displayed per kilogram, stood Nonno, Papa, Zio Lazio and my cousin Renaldo. That would be the first picture when I create an album of family photographs!

Meanwhile I set the insalata on the table where I dressed it with olive oil, red wine vinegar, salt, pepper and freshly picked oregano. As I tossed the salad and topped it with garbanzo beans, I hummed a tune I've heard my Papa sing often since I was a child. Whenever he played Enrico Caruso's album of Puccini's opera, *Tosca*, Papa would stop at Cavaradossi's heart-rending, *E lucevan le stelle* ...and the stars were shining. It was at this point he always sang most beautifully and clearly in harmony with Caruso.

Mamma removed cubes of cooked meat and portions of sausage from the delicious *suco* and placed the platter of meats in the oven to stay warm. She took my hand and placed it against her lovely soft cheek with its wet tracks of teardrops I had not noticed.

"Molto bello, molto bello!" were the first words she spoke. "*O dolci baci, o languide carezze!* (Oh, sweet kisses and languorous caresses), she sang to my humming, both of us aware this stunning aria, introduced by a somber clarinet, was Cavaradossi's last melodic wail as he waited for execution, his entire heart laid open with overwhelming love for life itself, and desperately in love with Tosca.

What would an opera be without a powerful villain and an extraordinarily desirable woman who resists his advances? Tosca is the beautiful soprano in love with Mario Cavarodossi, the artist. Baron Scarpia, Chief of Roman police, a noted tyrant, in a dramatic monologue, sings his scorn of the gentler arts of love, and boasts that he finds pleasure in ruthlessly possessing what he desires. In his private quarters, he tells Tosca her lover, Cavarodossi has been charged with treason and will be tortured and executed. She pretends that to save her lover's life she will allow Scarpia to have his way with her. Disingenuously, Scarpia commands his sycophant gendarme to stage a "mock" execution, while covertly referencing a previous ploy in which actual bullets are used. Tosca refuses Scarpia's declarations he will have her, and she stabs him. In the third act, while Cavaradossi awaits execution, Tosca rushes to tell her lover he should fake his death. Thus, neither of them feared the firing squad, until once she is left alone with his body, Tosca realizes the perfidious deception played on them. She throws herself over the roof parapet, and the curtain falls.

"Never have I loved life more..." Mamma sang on. I hung on her every syllable and note. She told me many times Papa sang this to her as she met him, leaving her brother's side, at the altar on their wedding day. Her brother Fabio acted as their Papa's surrogate, handing over the bride, his sister Angelina, to her beloved Carmine. "Papa just sang, unplanned, from the depths of his love for me. I was enraptured so thoroughly, I could neither hear nor see anything else besides this man whose love for me was so divine I would follow him anywhere."

We could hardly hold back tears, remembering Mamma's parents, sisters and other brothers had lost their lives in the tragic fire less than two years before her marriage to Papa. On her wedding day, they must have been present on her mind, until that very moment which she just described. Our breaths both deepened into a sigh, and quietly we resumed setting the table, holding the deeply shared moment between us, holding it to the end of our lives.

The neighbor's dog announced arrival of Nico and my Nonni, while Mamma and I shared a knowing smile and perked up for anticipated hugs, kisses and comments about how much I seemed to be growing and how splendid the kitchen smelled, while Nonna would fawn over the fresh dahlias, asters and ferns I had picked earlier. Nonna tasted the salad and nodded her approval while Mamma dropped fresh pasta into boiling salted water. Nico dashed into the bedroom to change into clean clothes from his work clothes, full of hay and chicken feathers accrued at our Nonni's neighbor's shack-like property.

Papa arrived to the clatter of dinnerware being set and wine being poured all around. We were aware this would be our final formal meal before the last preparations for our departure. The mood was happy, and abundant laughter poured across the table like wine into our glasses. Nonno sniffed the food audibly, placed his index finger pointing into his cheek like a pistol, turning back and forth and rolling his eyes toward heaven said, "*Che cuoca*" towards Mamma. "What a cook," his words encouraged us all to speak over each other as we plunged into the manicotti, pasta, insalata, and meats in their sauce still steaming from the oven. The traditional final touch was Mamma lavishing plenty of grated *Parmigiano formaggio*.

Despite Nonno's advanced years, he intended to manage the butcher shop, overseeing every aspect and employing nephews and cousins who so ably had been the backbone of the operation for as long as I could recall. Nonna would look after our home and rent it to newlyweds (some extended family, of course) after our departure. Without speaking directly of it, Nonna implied she would keep the grave sites of Mamma's premature twin babies respectfully and lovingly tended. Their precarious births at barely one kilo each had required emergency surgery, which left Mama unable to conceive more babies, but never to forget these she'd grieved over.

My Nonni brought over a steamer trunk, a gift from Monsignor Oliverio and nuns at the convent. Nonno said it was given to us as an expression of gratitude for blessings my family provided to parish clerics and sisters over many Christmases and Easters: lamb and ham roasts for which Papa never took any money, and frequent oxtail and neck bones for stews.

Papa leaned over to his papa and placed his hand over Nonno's. He spoke close and intimately as we all strained to hear. "Never, not ever will I forget your immense generosity. You gave it all -- teachings values and skills, patient disciplining to help us achieve better judgment, and modeling fatherhood and love." Breaking down while trying to speak, my Papa hesitated. The pause was not uncomfortable and may have lasted for less than a minute, but when he continued, his words broke from him. "Mamma and your children and grandchildren have been recipients of the most unselfish love imaginable. Papa, I'll do all I can to emulate that, *lo prometto*!" Papa's genuine promise, I can attest he kept.

Papa needed a few minutes to compose himself. In the next indelible moment, he resumed, "And more, I will always strive to bring honor to the Migliore name and legacy. You speak more carefully and far more elegantly than I've ever been able to do; you offer support even when not requested, and usually unspoken. You bring humor, honesty, loyalty and material gifts to us and to the community. Can you forgive me for abandoning you at this time?"

Nonno silently cried -- Mamma and Nonna did also -- and then their most heart-tugging gesture. He and Papa stood up and embraced, knowing they wouldn't see each other for a greater time than they could bear. I grabbed the camera and took more profoundly touching photos than I may ever have achieved since. How could I know then it would be nearly ten years before we would return for my Nonno's last days and leave my Papa and Mamma to stay on to take care of Nonna for her last years in Vietri.

Nonno's final words were for Salvatore, but I was not to know of their last, most private conversation until months after our arrival in Cordoba when Nico chillingly confided Nonno never regretted dragging him from joining the battles, but would always feel responsible for Nico's sometimes unrestrained anger.

Nonno begged Nico to learn to channel those feelings to make the world a better place. "You can do huge good where there is injustice, but never use means like those that have devastated our people. Never be the perpetrator of violence in any of its forms. Silence and neutrality allow hate to spread. We have activism in our blood and bones, we must use always for justice. Be a leader for those who are uncertain how to speak for themselves, who do not have a voice. Ours is not to seek vengeance, but justice. Believe me, Salvatore, I have found justice is evidence love prevails. Be true to these words and to yourself, and I will always have great pride in my heart for you."

I would see Nico evolve from the impetuous youth attempting to fight on the battlefield by any means, to a highly principled, incorruptible man sharing radical views of the anti-imperialist Argentinean, Che Guevara. Though short-lived, his friendship with Che remained one of the great influences on my brother's politics, values and activism. The effect on me was profound, and I too will always have great pride in my heart for my brother.

But I am getting ahead of myself. Justice is so central an issue and focus for me and my family, I cannot separate it from my other perspectives whether in my recollections or in my dealings as an adult.

EIGHT

---◆○◆---

September 4, 1947

CRIMES AGAINST HEAVEN

My memories of the last weeks prior to boarding the ship are replete with voids and inconsistencies, undoubtedly some protective mechanism my brain plays to handle my inability to accept a mostly unknown future. One thing stands out sharply, took place on the early morning we set out for Genoa to board the M.S. Vulcania.

My Nonni accompanied us, with a picnic basket of *sopprasotta* and Genoa sausages, two balls of provolone cheese, loaves of crusty fresh bread, jars of Nonna's canned pickled *giardiniera* of slivered garden vegetables, roasted red peppers, and my favorite, marinated eggplant. Accompanying these were dried figs strung in a circle, dried apricots, nuts, and two fruitcakes.

We were driven in the converted ambulance Monsignor Oliverio possessed for the purpose of transporting orphans, now in the care of parish nuns. War orphans. There were thousands across Europe, many of whom will never be re-united with parents. Lacking identification and unable to give more than a clue about where they were from, they would be difficult to place even if their families were alive to seek for them. I was like family to Adele and Adam, three- and five-year-old orphan siblings who clung to me every lunch time when I would arrive with Mamma and Nico for our Spanish lessons from Suora Ariana, youngest of the sisters at the convent. Their photos are amongst those currently on my third roll of film, pulling on Suora's habit playfully, wolfing down corn chowder and crusty bread at the long dining table, and hugging my leg to keep me from leaving. What age will they be when I return for a visit next? Will we recognize each other? Will they have been adopted or re-united with family?

Along the route our drive took to Genoa, we saw how little progress had been made in the reconstruction of Italy. Evidence of cities blasted to utter destruction by planes and tanks, coupled with continued shortages of food and supplies, was heartbreaking. Nonna begged to be allowed to offer coins, food, *anything* to the seriously underweight *ragazzi*, children who were living on the streets or begging for their displaced families who survived the war. We saw them everywhere: many destitute families with injuries, illness, poverty and trauma written on their faces, ragged clothing and barely cared-for bodies. Monsignor consolingly offered to say prayers and take up collections from our parish to distribute to these pitifuls.

Images of desolation and hopelessness were difficult to capture on camera...I wished never to see misery like that again. But I photographed rubble-strewn and battered neighborhoods, remnants from both the Germans' and the Allies' heavy bomb barrages, most during the period of Italy's civil war, 1943- 1945. One must wonder how these undernourished, displaced, damaged people would have strength and resources to rebuild? They hadn't even been able to clear away the debris of destruction surrounding them. Papa reached over and grabbed his mamma's hand and they both began to weep. "Mamma," he said, "it is hard to witness these scenes. This is the aftermath of Liberation. It will improve, though, no thanks to the Fascists who remain in positions of power in our country!" We drove in silence then, for hours it seemed.

Nico and I sitting on the trunks began teasing each other, breaking up the somber atmosphere. He grabbed the *salsiccia*, cured sausage, as if it was a billy club and raised it over his head threatening me, so I fended him off by squirting the seltzer bottle I found in the seat, aiming directly at his head. It was Papa this time who grabbed my camera and shot a picture. And then, of course, he told us to quit the antics! "*Abasta!*" he chuckled, poking Mamma in the ribs playfully, starting a poking war between them and infecting us with laughter.

Before we settled into our rooms at the convent, Monsignor Oliverio handed Mamma a beautifully carved wooden box. I recognized it for it contained the cherished statue of the Infant of Prague, centerpiece of the altar in my Nonni's cottage home. The ornate statue of infant Jesus dressed in a blue robe lovingly made by my Nonna, had golden brown locks and wore a gold crown. His left hand held a golden orb symbolizing kingship and right hand was raised with the palm in a blessing posture. Traditionally the eighteen-inch infant's clothes were routinely changed, coordinating embroidered robes and lace under-gowns to mark the holy days of Christmas, Easter, May Day, and the anniversary of my Nonni's wedding forty-five years ago. This statue had been a wedding gift from Nonno's parents to them and would now travel with us to Argentina. Mamma guarded this treasure through our entire travels and would create an altar in our new home for it, just like I had seen on every visit to my Nonni's.

This Infant's travel robe was a deep cerulean blue velvet with an undergarment made from Mamma's wedding veil of Venetian lace, handmade by Papa's godmother. That same veil is now a cherished heirloom Nonna preserved, hoping to see it grace my head on my wedding day. Strangely I was aware Monsignor held the statue as significantly more than a cherished family relic, but what that was would not be revealed to me until months later, when I discovered just how dangerous a treasure this child Jesus hid. Valuable and very dangerous for us!

"Remember my children, in all things, honor this blessed divine Child and you will never want. He will bless your family with peace and abundance," Monsignor spoke to Mamma as he blessed it again and handed it into her arms. We could never forget these words she repeated at every holy day of remembrance while she lit votive candles, and we knelt in prayer. There were more reasons Father Oliverio emphatically admonished us to remember, and I shudder to this day with what I didn't know then.

Waiting for us at the arranged time and place was our Zio Fabio. We had pre-arranged to meet at the convent in Genoa, at sunset the evening prior to our daybreak boarding the ship. Monsignor's friendly greeting the nuns and rectory priests clearly showed intimacy, when he introduced us to "my most trusted long-time friends."

Over a rather sumptuous dinner in the convent's elegant dining room, Monsignor explained he had been assigned to this parish in Genoa before being promoted to senior cleric in Vietri. But an uncomfortable conversation at the end of the table where he sat with this parish's senior clerics made me and Nico suspicious of less than cordial matters being discussed. What they might be about in such secretive, non-convivial discussions, became the focus of some uneasy conjecture Nico and I conveyed to Mamma that night.

Nico and I shared a sparsely furnished room next to our parents' identical room. After dinner, Nico and Zio Fabio delayed settling into their rooms, while I hung about Papa and Mamma's room. When he finally showed up, Nico addressed us in hushed tones, carefully selecting his words. "Often lately, I have felt Monsignor isn't being candid about what he is really about. Take this trip, for example, Papa. Was it really convenient timing for him to drive us on this date to Genoa? Julietta and I feel he's been contriving something circumspect and using our departure as an excuse to further a secret agenda."

Mamma's brows raised, her eyes darkened, and her breathing became faster and more pronounced. "Then I am not alone in picking up cues from his words, interactions, and evasiveness. How can we learn more? Is it beyond propriety to be suspicious? What evidence do we have of possible alternative intentions?"

I responded of my discomfort with Monsignor since the encounter in church when he seemed too eager to take over our plans for departure. I had felt jittery and suspicious with every plan he suggested to us. Nico sighed uncomfortably and added, "I didn't believe in Monsignor's benevolent facade and I'm now convinced of ill bodings in his scheming. Zio Fabio overheard the clerics discussing 'the papers' needed urgently by Cardinals who have convened in Genoa for the Vatican Diplomatic Corps. After dinner, Zio Fabio, with his espionage skills, steered me near their clan grouped just behind the wall east of the dining room. We heard talk of these papers, and an Argentinean diplomat who was to meet them at eight in the morning, of Perón's agents and Monsignor Montini, the pope's right-hand man, who will arrive by Vatican limousine from the Oriental Institute. Zio Fabio whispered they were speaking of a Vatican outpost where landing papers and Vatican stamped passports are prepared, illegally he is certain."

Mamma was shocked and asked Papa what sense he could make of these reports. He stroked her hand and suggested we sleep on it and discuss possibilities from that information. It was an uncomfortable, uneasy sleep for all of us.

At breakfast we shared our conflicted experience of distrust and dismay towards our host and 'spiritual leaders'. Zio Fabio confided there was indeed a conspiracy. He knew Nazis, the Vatican and Argentinean leaders have been providing safe passage for Nazi war criminals out of Europe to the same port at which we would be landing, Buenos Aires!

"Perón eagerly welcomes them, along with the gems, gold, and art they plundered throughout their conquests and brought to Argentinean markets. There those stolen treasures become source of support for high level Nazis, and other war criminals secreted out of Germany, where they otherwise would have likely faced prosecution, humiliation, and even execution. Probably every ship and plane leaving Europe this year has treasures to be smuggled into the hands of Perón, the Nazis and Fascists his network helped to flee."

"They may be carried by conspirators, moles, espionage agents, or trafficked by unsuspecting carriers. Maybe you'll even spot some suspicious activity aboard this ship. I'm certain there will be some!" Fabio laughed, breaking the tension of his words and allowing us to laugh, while maintaining an elevated level of suspicion.

NINE

THE SECRET SOLDIER

Now I must write about my mother's brother, Fabio. We held Zio Fabio dear to our hearts and adored any time we had the privilege of being with him. As her older brother and only other survivor of their family's tragic deaths, he took care of my Mamma until she reached adulthood and became Carmine's bride. Zio Fabio then enlisted into the Italian Alpine Corps where he rose quickly to become one of their most qualified mountaineering saboteurs. His value to us seemed to take second place to his value to our country.

Zio Fabio, tall, lean, handsome and arrogant, if that can be said of someone with a great sense of humor and jesting, was fiercely protective of his sister and us. Surely, he could not bear to lose another so dear to him. He and my Mamma, while visiting their mother's family in Vietri sul Mare, learned of the explosion and fire which took the lives of their entire remaining family, adjacent neighbors, homes and possessions. He admitted to us he had cried for weeks. Bleakness and depression so deeply consumed him, he took consolation from his sister, Angelina, and was ashamed afterward, feeling it should have been him consoling her.

My great uncle, Zio Leonardo, had driven them back to Bologna for the burial and memorial service provided by the Linguistics department where my nonno, Professor Salvatore Militello, had been an esteemed faculty member.

Zio Fabio resumed. "Leonardo took us to the Language Studies building which features a dedicated bronze memorial plaque created with his younger brother's name, honoring his service to Bologna, in perpetuity. The young Fascist rioters who were certain Professore Militello and his wife were harboring student agitators and seditionists, used explosives to kill their suspected enemy aides and serve as a warning to other academics. They were apprehended and beaten beyond recognition, as a warning to their compatriots. That horrific event, along with street clashes in succeeding weeks, was completely misreported in Mussolini's newspapers. It left many Italians suspicious of intellectuals and university students and faculty."

The photos and personal items from Nonno's office remain with Mamma and Fabio to treasure for generations. Our family visited this memorial plaque set into the stone entry of the Language Studies building on our only trip to Northern Italy just one year after the armistice was signed, while Papa's leg was healing. Papa wrapped his arms tightly around my sobbing Mamma as he told her his pains could never equate to the horror and pain he knew she experienced. Wiping her tears, he added, "God showed His merciful love by bringing us together in the bond of marriage and keeping me alive when so many were needlessly slain in the war involving the whole world." His embrace became another indelible memory, one which Nico later painted on canvas and framed to surprise them on their next anniversary.

On the Bologna visit, our family set aside despair of the deaths, set aside the pains and blames, paradoxical emotional lows and any misunderstandings. We were family again and loving the accounts shared by our enigmatic uncle. Zio Fabio's trademark statement (spoken in Spanish) was "This will sit very badly with the Maestro!" He believed the Spanish were less civilized but more fervent in the faith than Italians. In Italian he would pronounce the same statement, replacing "Master" (Maestro) with "Universe", referencing Galileo, who'd been convicted of heresy as a result of declaring his conviction the sun, and not the earth, was at the center of our solar system.

"The Holy Church held with certainty all the universe revolved around our planet. After all, God's greatest creation, man, inhabited earth. It was man's domain and thus could not be lesser than any other."

In front of Bologna's Basilica di San Petronio, a Gothic basilica with a strangely unfinished brick and marble facade (the 14th century church ran short of funds for the marble?) after Sunday mass, Captain Fabio spoke loudly enough to turn heads, "We are expected to believe in infallibility of the Pope. That's as great a joke as believing Mussolini and Hitler were military and political geniuses! Oh, the stories I'll tell once the oath of secrecy I have sworn gets lifted!" We were the only ones laughing with him, while the devout streaming past us looked with disdain. There he stood in military uniform, equating those despised dictators with their venerated Pope!

We wandered onto Piazza Maggiore, strolling the grand square bordered by arcades in classical style with arched colonnades, bell towers and the statue of Neptune prominently visible, in all his naked lordliness. "This massive fountain features the God of the Sea, trident in hand. Neptune holds his hand out as if to calm the waters, the ultimate symbol of power. But the original version of this monument to power may have been a bit **too** powerful. According to legend, sixteenth-century sculptor, Giambologna, was commissioned to construct a fountain to symbolize the Pope's power and reign, ruler of land, like Neptune ruled oceans. Pope Pius IV, concerned by the manliness of Neptune, ordered the genitals made smaller.

Before you snicker, hear the rest of the story!" Fabio spoke as if he was a tour guide and continued.

"Because you don't say no to the Pope, Giambologna grudgingly obliged, but secretly got his revenge. While standing behind and to the right of the statue, observers might notice Neptune's hand is extended in a particular way. His thumb pokes out past his leg, creating an illusion the god seems very ... excited ... indeed. One need only look down at the statue's shadow (at the right time in the afternoon) to confirm the sea god's firmness and virility. Our Italian word "*furbo*" handily suggests the cunning attribute of artists like this sculptor!" Once again, Zio Fabio's hearty laugh turned heads and caused me to blush.

Fabio added,"Another story has been passed down of our celebrated Michelangelo, while creating a statue of Pope Julius II who commissioned it, was given such meager quarters he had to sleep four to a bed with his workmen. And, it should be noted, he was an unsociable person. The Vatican hardly can be commended for its treatment of the greats!"

Mamma and Zio Fabio began to reminisce about their youth in this ancient city as we dined at Caffe Vittorio Emmanuele, a meal I recall, being considerably different from our Southern Italian favorites. A sampling included: Mortadella, baloney's predecessor, sweet, delicately spiced, and bigger than your head. We're talking about Prosciutto from Parma, Coppa from Piacenza, and Parmigiano Reggiano from Modena. Capping it off was panna cotta for me and Nico! Tio Fabio our connoisseur, touted local wine favorites: Sangiovese, Pignoletto and the classic red sparkler Lambrusco. "Unlike the swill passed off as imported Italian vino, available in grocery stores around the world, the excellent Lambrusco produced in Emilia-Romagna pairs perfectly with Bologna's hearty pasta fare. Tortellini en brodo, veal cottolletii (cutlet) and pasta Bolognese, a meat ragu, are served tonight family style, compliments of your favorite spy!" Zio Fabio could be counted on to exaggerate and jest, so we were left to speculate further about his self-description.

As Captain Fabio M. Militello, he had commandeered a first-class military jeep along with a four-day leave allowing him to stay with us through our ship's departure and then return my Nonni to the Genoa station for their train to Naples. He boldly drove us right up to the passenger loading platform, abruptly stopping closer than any other vehicle for our first view of our ship and fellow passengers. "*O Mio Dio*!!" gasped Nonna at the ship's size and magnificence.

The M.S. Vulcania was an elegant ocean liner newly retrofitted for transatlantic passenger travel after six years of serving wartime shipping needs. Celebrating her maiden post-war voyage was the Mayor of Genoa, a large number of dock workers, photojournalists, media reporters and masses of friends and kin of departing passengers. Horns, confetti, flags waving, and marching bands greeted us as we boarded. Throngs at the dock included thousands of other Europeans, most of whom would similarly be settling in for a new life on a new continent. The journey would take nearly two weeks. I was not going to be rushed as I shot more than a dozen photos, mostly posed, all with our ship in the background. Due to post-war shortage of paper, we hadn't been given a brochure full of enticing pictures of the M.S. Vulcania. I'd seen ads in Life magazine featuring this ship and her sister ocean liner the Saturnia – poster-type photos showing the outside but lacking interior photos. I could feel my heart thumping with anticipation!

Papa grabbed me about my waist, and while he lifted me into the air, I saw we shared the same awestruck expression of utter childlike glee. "It's our new beginning, my love," Papa said. "We are the most fortunate family with so much ahead for us. God knows we've suffered enough, and He is providing us a reward! Time to board!"

The massive ship was amazing and stepping aboard lifted our mood. My family stood together behind the deck railing to watch departure from the dock and my Nonni, until we were far from sight. Nonna held her empty arms out; Nonno wiped at tears flowing. They never turned away. I set my packages at my feet and clicked pictures through tears of my own sure I heard their voices, *"Buon voyagio, I miei preziosi!"* Final wishes for a good voyage for their precious ones still make my eyes sting whenever I recall their last words.

Mamma was inconsolable faced with departure from her big brother Fabio. With eyes cast down she spoke only five words," Is this the right thing?"

Nico took her hand and then wrapped his arms around her waist and answered, "Yes, Mamma. It is the right thing." He held her while she sobbed, until Papa put his arms around both of them, pushing her chin up for *un baccio precioso.* I still have the treasured photo of that precious kiss.

TEN

••••••◆○◆••••••

September 4 1947

JOURNEY TO A NEW WORLD

T he captain and crew members introduced themselves and distributed schedules and instructions to the travelers watching the Ligurian seacoast and clutching their young children. I remember pondering the Port of Buenos Aires might be even larger than the Port of Genoa, and appreciating the vastness of the ocean. My excitement was climbing and my heart racing. New clothes, gifts from Papa's brothers' families, lovingly stitched for me, were itchy and definitely not warm enough! Mamma settled the new angora cape she made for this voyage around my too thin shoulders and I gasped the cool morning air while tossing my head back! Looking back ten years ago now, I vividly recall the splendor to all my senses as we glided across rich hues of blue sea on that glorious late summer morning. Passengers were obviously enthused to embark upon a multitude of new experiences and the laughter and spontaneous joy was contagious! Music played, couples danced, and children – well, they clapped and played!

It had been more than 8 ominous and too often miserable years since war began. Final views of our homeland were filled with the ecstasy of its splendor. Italy is profoundly beautiful, and richly blessed with culture, history and the most wonderful, generous people in the world. Lucky for my family, we would have not only our own Italian family to embrace in Argentina, but would be surrounded by Italians like us.

That's all I knew except what my cousins had written about their friends from Brazil, Spain, France, Germany and Britain. Their school was more a gathering of cultures than was their neighborhood, called a *barrio*. Students there take a *collectivo*, a bus which collects them from many *barrios* and takes them to a school near the urban center, surrounded by public buildings and elegant homes of high social class families. When Zio Paolo came back to gather his family and their belongings for departure to Argentina, he brought issues of Life Magazine featuring pictures of the many faces of Argentina, people whose faces I studied for their glorious refinement, or conversely for their impoverished, undernourished, usually dark-skinned oddness. The regalia of the powerful was in opposition to the meanness of the powerless; and you could pick out the healthful, seemingly prosperous middle class of mostly European descent, usually walking to jobs on fabulous European style streets in Buenos Aires. Zio Paolo's photographs of the meat packing factory and his fellow workers looked nothing like any I had seen, even in Naples. Relatives, friends, neighbors, everyday life for him hardly seemed Italian at all!

A commotion on deck returned me to our journey as I pivoted towards the organ grinder and his small monkey entertaining all on their approach. The monkey was dressed in a skirt of red, green and white ribbons and tulle netting, like worn by a bride to fluff out her gown below the waist. The little capuchin held out a cup to collect coins from delighted families. The musician played and sang "Mezzaluna" and "I Cuori", and promised to return later to play the "Tarantela" for which the monkey named Barbara would lead us in a dance!

Papa had been handed name tags on lanyards for each of us, including group assignments and the name of the steward for our group. Our family was one of twelve, grouped in the Azure Seas designation; we noticed other group names like White Gulls, Red Sunsets, and Golden

Sunrise. Pietro Bagnifredo, assigned to the Azure Seas group, had memorized familial names, the number in their families, name of the Signora, and the cabin he had prepared expressly for them! He was charming but less than handsome with a cleft palette and trimmed mustache, and he exuded attentiveness and politeness that put us at ease. Pietro assured everyone in our group, as we created a human rosette, there would be absolutely no chaos under his watch, and we could summon him for any concern! I counted four babies in their mamma's arms, easily fifty children, mostly well behaved, and a diverse retinue amongst us. Hoping I wasn't drawing attention to myself, I read name tags, last names first in bold capital letters, then first names. Parents also had their children's names written under their own.

Zio Fabio had taught us phrases in German, English and Spanish so I was comfortable with pronunciation of Braun, Miller, Valencia, and Weiss. Since the remaining seven families were Italian, I didn't need to practice their names. We all smiled, spoke the common English "Hello" greeting as prompted by Pietro and then, at his further instruction, followed him to the Grand Ballroom. I heard gasps from most passengers in our 2nd class group, "cabin class". First class accommodations would surely be pretty fancy if the splendor of this enormous ballroom with its gilded metal staircase was any indication! The architects of the ship's interior must have visited the great cathedrals, magnificent churches and the Vatican itself for inspiration! I recall being awestruck while on a holiday visit to Naples of the monumental beauty of Gesu Nuovo Church, the Monumental Complex Donnaregina and the Duomo! That such grandeur would have been created in tribute to God and the saints seemed a more profound purpose than to be provided for the pleasure of the few who could afford first class accommodations aboard an ocean liner. Moreover, it must account for this ship being called a "Superliner" with its smokeless diesel engines, large stack positioned at midship, ability to travel up to 21 knots, and carry over 500 first and second class, 320 third class, 1350 fourth class and a crew of 440!

The description Mamma read from her inquiries at the travel agency in Naples prepared me, but everything resplendent seemed also grandly exaggerated and pompous. "Magnificent and lordly as Versailles, the palace of the Sun King, Louis XIV and his wife Marie Antoinette. First-class passengers also have an indoor swimming pool, a sumptuous reproduction of the magnificent Pompeian bath." I repeated these memorized phrases to Nico, who commented we'd better take it all in now, since we were certainly not going to see those wonders once we were herded out of the Grand Ballroom.

Pietro gathered us closely, aware he needed to be heard, but not overheard by other groups. "The most important information, I will tell you first. Safety is number one at all times! In just a few minutes the ship's captain will welcome all of you with an introductory statement about himself, the crew, and some pre-departure wisdom." Pietro gave a shy laugh then went on. "Each family has been given packets with explicitly detailed maps of the entire ship as well as another map of areas you will use, depending on the class of steerage; specific seated dining room schedules, emergency instructions and more is awaiting your studious review. Until we hear chimes announcing an important message from the captain, you can get to know each other, okay? Then all must pay attention, please!"

The smiles and chatter were, at first, inhibited but members of our group seemed to have little hesitation to reveal their stories, once initial pleasantries were exchanged. Albert and Marta Weiss, standing alongside my family had three children, but they looked nearly too young to have children at all. The Valencia family of five were extremely handsome with their black Spanish hair and eyes and their elegant clothes of fine fabrics, tailored for the latest fashion; The Millers, the Abrahams and the Brauns were more subdued but personable, and clearly the language barrier between Germanic and Romance-based languages could have been the reason for their being aloof. Cultural differences between Germans, Italians and Spanish might account for their seeming lack of warmth. We'd learn more over the next dozen days as these would be our dining room partners.

Just as the oldest daughter of Fritz and Arlene Braun approached me with a smile, we heard chimes to quiet occupants of the ballroom. Once the captain had completed his welcome message, some beautiful romantic strains played over the loudspeaker, providing a soft ambience to relax us back to conversations. Pietro broke in, sweetly asking for our attention, as soon he would be providing a guided tour of our cabin class facilities. "We call this ship a luxury ocean liner, as she has been made to afford the greatest comforts of any sailing vessel since pre-war glories of Atlantic crossings. It will be necessary to become familiar with some terms, like aft, which is rear of the ship, and bow, which is front of the ship. Port refers to left side of the ship when facing the bow, and starboard is right side. The very back is the stern and decks are divided into three levels, with cabin class having the entire second level for your daily promenades and exercises to keep you in shape during our passage. The Lido has a swimming pool, verandas, chairs and chaises you will never tire of -- I guarantee! Waiters will be taking your drink and snack requests from the comfort of the Lido deck starting after breakfast hour throughout the day and into evening, unless seas are too rough, or skies are dumping too much rain. Blankets and towels are abundantly provided as well!"

"Now, please follow as I show you other features, ending at the Lido. You have a map of the ship and more maps can be found midship, the middle of the ship, of course, between the purser and the activities director's offices. We will not have occasion to ascend the Grand Staircase in the atrium on this voyage, but who knows? Maybe you will take a return voyage in the future and enjoy first-class suites." Pietro's voice remained pleasingly audible, and his Italian accent was beautiful. His German and Spanish must have been good as he repeated everything in three languages!

We walked into the dining room with its round tables and leather chairs, ornate columns and handsome wood paneling from floor to ceiling, amazingly decorated with majolica tiles in colors reminiscent of my own hometown. There were fresh flowers on each table here and in the Smoking Room and the Bar, with its Persian rug, Vestibule with its oversized upholstered chairs and sofas, Reading and Writing room with a library, and Music room with its drums, piano, stage, and potted palms. No hotel I could imagine would even compare! As our troop exited to the Lido deck, brilliant sunlight and azure blue skies flooding us, the surrounding sea was as captivating as I imagined and views of Italy's western coast were a marvel. Picture time!

Papa seemed immobile until pushed lightly by Mamma, who suggested we prepare ourselves for lunch, as we must be seated promptly at 11:30. Sunlight had warmed the decks but cabins and dining room felt chilly to me, so I remained in the clothes that I first walked onto the gangplank wearing, while others shed their sweaters. I'm used to everyone else in my family being hardier than me, but I knew the moment I could get out to the Promenade I would welcome warmth for hours.

Placards at each table setting provided a formal seating arrangement, with some of our adjacent dining companions speaking Italian and others speaking German. I found it clumsy, but it would just take some getting used to as no one else seemed to have been in this circumstance before. That's when I heard Marta Weiss speaking Italian to Mamma who sat next to her. Mamma, clearing her throat, said, "I'm pleased to hear your fluidity in Italian. My German is inadequate, and my Spanish is still in the learning stage. May I introduce my family?"

From that point on, they spoke familiarly, and we learned Marta and Albert had met while students at the University of Bologna and eloped early in their undergraduate careers. Marta's maternal aunt had moved from Munich, their hometown, to Bologna to care for the children who arrived all within the first five years of their marriage. Shyly, Marta retold the story of great-aunt Leona pondering to them her concern they need not re-populate Germany or Italy after the war. Albert firmly denied so, while Aunt Leona and Marta had a good laugh. "You see, Leona felt she was fleeing the terrors and cruelty of Germany and its people for greater civility in Italy. There we were, all six of us in Bologna where horrendous bombing and tank battles took place the last year of the war. Yet, thanks to her, Albert and I both completed our university degrees, his in engineering and mine in music theory. Great Aunt Leona wanted to make this trip with us, but instead she compassionately brought my parents from Germany to live in our apartment. Thankfully, nobody questioned our decision to leave, nor asked for our assurance we would return. We simply will not." Marta looked determinedly at Albert with her declaration.

"On our part," Mamma spoke, aware Albert and the couple next to him were also listening, "We left what had been a blessed life in Vietri sul Mare, near Salerno, feeling God had turned His back on us. There, surrounded by most of my husband Carmine's family, and their thriving butcher business, our hopes and dreams were shattered after so many years of war, and Carmine's near death on the battlefield fighting alongside the Allies. Carmine's brother started a new life eight years ago in Cordoba and we're glad he booked passage for us to enable us to do the same."

Marta, holding the baby on her lap while urging the other two children to finish their soup, managed to keep chatting with Mamma. "You say you are from Southern Italy and yet your dialect sounds much like the Bolognese dialect. Am I being too forward in asking about that?"

Mamma answered her, "I guess someone whose study was music theory would have a good ear for nuances and peculiarities, even dialects. There are so many throughout Italy. I have family roots in Vietri sul Mare, but I had spent my early life in Bologna where my father was head of the university Linguistics department and my mamma was an important part of university life. They perished with my siblings when an explosion destroyed their home. I was visiting Vietri with my brother at the time. It was Carmine's love that carried me through that horror. We married about two years later."

"My only surviving brother, Fabio is a Captain in the Italian Special Forces, stationed in their alpine division, near Turin. His fluency with languages brought notice from the higher military echelons, so his military career began with intensive training to be a member of Special Forces, and as a paratrooper he has worked his way up the ranks."

Mamma realized she was bragging and remarked with a sigh, "I don't feel right leaving behind all the family members and friends who have sacrificed and suffered alongside us. I feel certain we will return many times. Our permanent new home will be Argentina, but my heart will remain divided between our home countries, in the old and new world."

Another Italian mother at the table leaned in toward us and shared her truth. "We all have tragedies to put behind us. We all have new hopes and dreams for our lives in Argentina. Maybe we can drink a toast to the joys of better days at tonight's dinner?" The adults agreed and resumed eating plates of fresh fruits and sandwiches. Lunch was served buffet style, with selections of lunch meats, cheeses, breads and rolls, pepperoncini, olives, sliced carrots and fennel, perfect tomatoes, fruits and juices to choose from. There was a separate table just for desserts. I won't even go into descriptions of those, but at least three flavors of gelato caught my eye along with devil's food cake with fudge icing and on and on.

Nico snuck an extra sandwich back to the room, eating it while we dressed in our bathing attire. He snapped the back of my swimsuit causing me to circle around him and pull up on the back of his swim trunks. I laughed so hard, I had to gag myself to stop. Nico just retorted, "I'll get you back when you least expect it. Count on it!"

I barely filled out Mammas' bathing suit from four years ago when her irregular eating and worries caused significant weight loss. Mamma now has a strikingly beautiful figure, and in her new bathing suit of maroon with a wide white strip across her bosom, I would notice heads turn!

From behind, strong, masculine arms enfolded a surprised Mamma as Papa brushed his lips against her hair, her cheek and then lightly on her lips, saying in a seductive, amorous voice, "So this is what is meant by *La Vida Far Niente*, the pinnacle of Italian joy. The good life of doing nothing!"

Mamma whispered something in his ear and he drew in a deep breath, then said, "I can hardly wait, *mi amore*." I heard him softly sing to her those same words he had sung to her on their wedding day, "Never have I loved life more..."

ELEVEN

---◆◇◆---

BETWEEN TWO WORLDS

There was bustling and confusion while cabins were located, with instructions to be shipside in 30 minutes for life-saving instructions broadcast in 3 languages. My family's cabin was small with only a matrimonial bed for two and bunk beds, one for Nico who claimed the lower bed and one for me, glad to be in the upper bunk. The cabin had four chairs around a table which could barely fit four salad size plates and water glasses. But no matter, as those seats provided a view of the ocean through the porthole. Beds were covered in new white linens with white chenille coverlets, red woolen blankets at the foot, and feather pillows plumped up and immensely comfortable! On Mamma's pillow was a single red rose Mamma kissed and then placed in a glass of water in the center of our tiny table, while giving orders to us. "Each of us gets one drawer under her bed and 3 hangers in the closet. Figure out what you will wear for the first part of our trip and unpack those first. Pajamas under the pillows, robes on the hooks and slippers next to the door, ready to replace shoes when we enter."

"*Abasta!*" instructed Papa in a soldierly fashion. Stealing a look at Nico, I giggled and hurried to beat him to our bunkbed so I could dangle my feet over my claimed loft while he was still unpacking.

Mamma was delighted by the rose scented shampoo and soaps provided in a bathroom so small you really could barely turn around if you were standing at the sink. There was no shower door, but only a barely adequate curtain, and the toilet was between the shower and sink with a pull flush that made a huge gushing sound. Hopefully it would be rarely used during long nights at sea! Speaking about being at sea, Papa volunteered should we have rough waves, the same sex parent and child would have to hold onto its counterpart when showering, especially when trying to wash one's hair.

"Thanks for the instructions, Carmine. Now I comprehend why there are rails on all the beds!" laughed Mamma. "Time to get on deck." I grabbed my camera and followed her lead.

By our third day out at sea (Oh, I loved that term!), we felt comfortably familiar with the assignments, layout and routines. Deck hands in their navy jackets, white pants and shoes stood out among colorful passengers, encouraging intermingling. Verla Braun acted like befriending me was her priority, I assumed because we were very similar in age. After some obvious positioning where she would come over and join me whenever she saw me with Nico, I recognized flirtation was her intention. Not that Nico minded -- he was more charming than I recall with friends he hung around with back home. Eventually, she gave up the ploy of seeking me out, and hastened to join him whenever there might be a "chance" encounter. Nico decided he ought to learn German, which caused Papa to laugh into his ice water, making it spill out between his teeth, and we giggled at Nico's blushing.

I found I enjoyed playing with Marta and Albert's children as I had always enjoyed my young cousins. They had a trunk full of games, books and stuffed toys, a bigger cabin, and a surprising number of rather nice outfits. There was a small treasure box I noticed Marta hide when I first entered their cabin to babysit the children one late afternoon. She brushed it off saying it held letters from her family she held dear, but it seemed strange to me. If they were refugees, how do you account for the obviously upper income which had afforded these and the upgraded ocean crossing passage *we* could not have afforded, despite my family's relative prosperity in Vietri?

Mrs. Weiss might have told Mamma something which would explain this. They are often deep in conversation. I have even seen them go off to the chapel to pray together! Mrs. Weiss did not seem at all as fervent in her Catholicism as my relatives; there was a furtiveness about her gazes, a vulgarity in her speaking, and I never saw her with a rosary of even a cross. Blasphemy or cultural irregularity?

The evening of our sixth night out of port, the younger steward, who turns the head of every woman aboard, approached Mamma and me as we stood on the foredeck looking out on the setting sun. "*Buonasera, le miei belle donne!*" Gio spoke to us, "his beautiful women", with a sweep of his hat as he bowed. "How can I serve you? Would you like your picture taken with that amazing camera? I know how to take very sharp photographs, and in fewer than 10 minutes our ship will be encountering a sister ship. With that ship as a backdrop in the setting sun, *Mio Dio*! I'm now handing out flags which, by tradition, we wave while both ships' horns fill the air." He returned to us after using a bull horn telling other passengers he would be passing out flags, or they could just wave their hands at the approaching ship.

"When we cross the equator, we hold a ceremony at the swimming pool in recognition of the crossing. We'll enjoy "Big Band" swing music and encourage everyone to dance -- offering dance instruction as well! Julietta, would you be my partner as I teach the passengers? I can teach you the moves of modern dance over the next few days if you will allow me the honor! And Signora Migliore, I would be honored to teach you, as well, of course!"

Mamma and I exchanged glances, and both piped in our eagerness to be participants. Then, oddly, Gio asked us if we were happy to be re-uniting with our friends from Bologna, the Weiss family. "The kindly monsignor singled me out from the crew members the day before our departure, and mentioned your families should be seated at the same dining table, as you are both friends of his, I supposed. But then I saw how well you get along and I guessed you already knew each other. That must be so sweet! Excuse me, I am being called by the gentlemen over there, who probably want to have me fetch their wives to participate in the event."

Mamma asked me if he could be mistaken, and I nodded my certainty he was speaking the truth. "I don't think Monsignor expected Gio to even mention this, Mamma. Don't you think it is one more oddity which adds to the other "unplanned coincidences", and should make us truly suspicious. What possible reason would Monsignor have for assuring we meet our "old acquaintances"? As for the Weiss family, I have additional concerns."

I couldn't finish my words, let alone my thoughts for at that moment the steward rushed us into picture taking position as the ships blasted their horns, everyone on the decks waved, and the setting sun brought coolness to the open deck, forcing us to grab for our sweaters. Papa and Nico had been swimming and were both jolted by the horn blasts. They wrapped towels around themselves and joined us to watch the sun setting. We spoke of the odd mention of re-uniting with the Weiss family, causing Papa and Nico to look at us quizzically.

Nico piped in he doesn't believe in coincidences, and we should be cautious about what we tell anyone, especially Marta and Albert. "They conveniently know Monsignor? And yet they failed to mention this to us? Zio Fabio needs to learn about this -- he's well equipped to investigate connections or suspicious activities and we've already been discussing the clerics' possible interventions to provide passports and papers to get high level Nazis out of Europe. This must be connected!"

Papa held Mamma at arms' length and asked her pointedly what she might have discussed with Marta that could be useful to Monsignor and other covert parties. Shaking slightly, she replied she could think of nothing except personal shares, future plans, and children. "Angelina, what questions did she have for you? Did you mention my active role in the resistance? Did you tell her about being delivered to Genoa by Monsignor and our concerns there might be some extra-legal activities being planned? Did you mention your brother Fabio and his position in the Special Operatives Intelligence? Think, Angelina! Anything could be of crucial importance!"

With tears starting in her eyes, Mamma asked us to please talk about this in our cabin, as Marta has habitually been seeking her out for a deck walk after putting the children down for the night. "She will know something is out of kilter if I am in this state of uncertainty and holding out concerns. Carmine, maybe you should answer her knock by saying I need some extra rest."

Nico and I literally held our breaths waiting for Mamma to speak. "I rarely get friendly with anyone, but Marta and her family seemed so eager and interesting, and they shared so many of my interests. Oh, what have I done? I don't really know them at all, but I trusted Marta as if she were family! Oh, my God, what have I done?"

I wrapped my arms around her and swayed her to relative calm, while Papa sat across the room and wiped perspiration off his forehead. His reassuring words, "I know you have done nothing to implicate us or place us in danger, *mi amore*, so don't be upset. A spirit like yours is all about healing, compassion and trust, and I wouldn't have you change any aspect of who you are. There cannot be anything for us to fear, even if you told them something which inadvertently provided spurious evidence. We aren't players in any conspiracy, and none of us will let on we are aware of something causing us to be suspicious."

Nico suggested, "Maybe you can feed some inaccurate information in response to her inquiries, misleading her so we can discern what she is really seeking. You can even plant something in your conversation about Monsignor and get her to wonder what that is about. Mamma, you have kept secrets from Julietta and me in the past, quite successfully!"

Mamma still held onto me as she responded, "OK, now I am composed again, I will confess to having shared with Marta about how we arrived at the decision to leave our hometown and about plans we have for our new life in Cordoba. She was so eager to learn more about Cordoba and our Italian family there and expressed optimism they might also be settling in Cordoba. You know Albert is an engineer. Well, there is an aeronautical factory and training school in

Cordoba, where she said Albert has been asked to consider taking a position. It sounded so perfect. I guess, too perfect."

Nico and I nodded agreement. Mamma seemed even more dismayed as she continued, "I bragged about my brother Fabio, too. But I gave her no reason to think of him as a spy. I spoke of his well-deserved position in the paratrooper division of Italian Special Operations. And, I'm ashamed to admit, I told her he had been one of the operatives planning the escape route for downed Allies to find their way back to the front after 1943. *O Mio Dio*, what have I done?"

In the cabin, Nico whispered, after discussing these revelations we should spend some time in the game room, giving our parents time alone, maybe for several hours.

"Mamma, Nico spoke softly to her, "You and Papa should spend some time figuring out what may be going on and a plan for us to respond without giving away our suspicions. I trust the two wisest people I know will arrive at a great decision. So, I'm taking Julietta off to the game room for a rousing game of Parcheesi. We'll be back before bedtime at 11 pm."

Nico could be perceptive and mature when the occasion calls for it, I thought. Winking at him, I assented and we walked together, closing the cabin door.

Angelina

After Nico and Julietta left for the game room, Carmine and I wasted no time closing in the space of intimacy that was left. He nuzzled, then kissed me as we discarded our clothes, and our lovemaking was both passionate and endearing. We made love a second time, consumed with only each other, with no other desire than from the sparks ignited whenever his lips brushed my nipples and devoured my neck and my mouth. I became the playful partner so engaged in arousing him and getting lost in the passions he aroused in me. It was all the existence we could endure or imagine.

"Angelina," Carmine spoke softly, while I lay sprawled half atop his nakedness. "When Father Oliverio asked if I, Carmine, would take you, Angelina, to be my lawfully wedded wife, to have and to hold from this day forward, all I could think, past the lump in my throat and the tears running down my face, was 'Angelina'! A gift from the angels, now *my* Angelina! And I would be your protector for life. So, I always speak and think your name as a whole, just as I adore you as a whole."

Softly touching Carmine's cheek with my long fingers, I replied, "And you, Carmine, give me the strong sense of being rooted to this earth, while soaring with angels. Forever I will follow you anywhere. Forever I will allow you to provide me peace, security, and protection. *Te adoro, mi amore.*"

We showered playfully, decided talk of this evening's portentous concerns could wait for morning, and lay together for a peaceful sleep, barely interrupted, even when our children returned for the night.

TWELVE

●●●●◆○◆●●●●

DISPOSABLE TRUTHS

Morning came too soon. "We need to create a plan", Mamma said as she roused us, "consistent with our friendly relationships while taking precautions to reveal nothing which can arouse the suspicions of the Weiss family or anyone on this ship for that matter. With all we are piecing together, we are wise to keep track of conjectures and unsettling experiences. But we know of no purpose for our family to be complicit in covert, possibly Fascist plans. Look at me -- I appear as happy and carefree as usual. Only now, I intend to set up some traps while pretending complete oblivion."

While placing my nightgown under my pillow, I asked, "Mamma, are you aware the Weiss family has some significant source of income? Mrs. Weiss never mentioned any source of wealth, inheritance or other fortune to you, did she? In fact, she gave us the impression they were a struggling post-graduate couple with three children to manage. Seems the truth is quite the opposite. Didn't you also notice the much larger cabin they have secured? I have seen trunks filled with newer clothing and toys, and the beautifully carved "treasure" box Mrs. Weiss locked and stowed away when I came to look after her children. As she was whisking the box away, she made sure to tell me it was for treasured letters and mementos from her family. Yet, she never seems fond enough of them to give more than a mention. You have precious letters, mementos and your treasured statue of the child, Jesus, but have never locked nor hidden them."

Responding to my new revelation, Mamma said, "I need to ponder, so I might find a way to have her reveal what we suspect, she is more than she has so far admitted to being. I'm quite curious about what is in that box she locks and hides away. Maybe she is stowing treasures as part of the Nazi escape strategy Fabio has been privy to learning about? I wasn't comfortable with his intimations, so I asked him directly to tell me all he could about this quasi-true, quasi-fictional story. Before I reveal what he told me -- and made me swear not to reveal -- I want to know about any other encounters or comments that might confirm our suspicions."

Papa was first to describe his observations the Weiss family seemed to conveniently fit in so well with us, but rarely had much to do with Germans or Northern Italians with whom they'd surely have more in common. He also noticed the Braun family was circumspect and guarded, rarely joining in activities, instruction or classes, adding "with the exception of Verla, who is a vivacious darling, nothing like the rest of her family. But then, I am sure you've noticed that, right Nico?"

"No kidding around, Papa. I've reluctantly entertained her now and then, but she's just such a phony. However, she has talked about her parents' wishing they could have stayed in Berlin and been part of both rebuilding and the expected new prosperity once industry was back to pre-War levels. She is sure the world would come to see German people were not in agreement with Hitler's "final solution" and racist hatred. Verla insisted Germans are really kind, using her family and grandparents as an example. I just scratched my head and looked over at them on their deck chairs with towels shielding their eyes and was unconvinced. I asked her what she was leaving behind, and she brusquely replied, "Nothing. Why?"

When it was my turn, I said I would keep my eyes and ears open, my mouth shut and use my camera should I notice anything worth recording. Then, I suggested we learn what Mamma knew before we all went to breakfast. I moved towards the cabin door, making hand signals to get the rest of the group out for the day. I was looking forward to devouring another sumptuous breakfast, and felt we could talk more as we walked to the dining room.

As we walked closely, Mamma quietly told us the shocking secret Zio Fabio entrusted to her, more stinging details about the role of our church in providing a safe destination where vicious enemies responsible for the war that turned the world on its head could hide to escape justice.

"The Vatican itself, with fervent assistance of its trusted clerics and allies in Switzerland, Germany, Spain, Italy and now the eastern Soviet Bloc, has been providing safe passage to high level Nazis since the United States joined the Allies, and it became apparent Germany would not be victorious against the Reds on the east and the Allies, including Italy, on all other fronts. None could ever convince Hitler of Germany's mistakes and defeat, so most of his upper level command, SS, and murderous war criminals hoarded treasures of art, jewels, gold and cash from their Jewish victims and others sent to their concentration camps. The Nazis are avowedly anti-Communist, exactly the type of henchmen useful to achieve the Holy Church's goals of preventing Soviet Bolshevism, Communism and even, God help us, Liberalism from becoming dominant forces in the governments newly emerging."

Papa joined in, "I believe all of this, and it's making me so totally angry I want to lash out! What makes anyone think we would play any part in this? What part is Monsignor Oliverio expecting us to play? How will Fabio uncover these possibly wicked intentions?"

"Fabio", Mamma assured us, "will stop at nothing to prevent these escapes and also to keep us safe." At that, we followed her into the dining room, deeply troubled, and with an easily explained loss of appetite.

The rest of the journey was fun, despite the queasiness and distrust we could not shake. It tempered our outgoing, easy friendliness, but we couldn't let that show. We had to become skilled at espionage, diversions, and pretense of innocence. It was less of a challenge once we set ourselves to uncovering what lay hidden, probably right in front of us.

The day before we were to arrive in Buenos Aires began with every new friend made aboard ship discussing their anticipated days and months ahead, and exchanging addresses where each might stay in contact by letter writing at least. Mamma had written cards for the Weiss family and the Brauns, with the address where Zio Paolo had leased a home for our family. Each of these families had done the same for us, with their anticipated address initially, at least. Verla Braun sweetly handed hers to Nico with an address in Buenos Aires, saying her father's sister was living in this mansion on Calle Huntington and would be welcoming her family to occupy the entire third floor. She was to be enrolled in a private Catholic academy and her mother would take up a teaching position in that same school. She added it would be their pleasure to have us visit soon, hopefully. I guess she assumed Cordoba was a suburb of Buenos Aires rather than the next largest city in Argentina 400 miles to the northwest.

Marta, Albert, Georgy, and Vanna, strolling baby Leo, acted rather nervous for the first time in our presence. When we looked at their address, it was at a hotel in Cordoba, not Buenos Aires as we had initially heard from them. "What's this?" Mamma asked when she saw they now were certainly headed to our very same destination. "How amazing you made this decision within the last few days? And what of your plans to live in the swanky Buenos Aires neighborhood where your 'distant' brother-in-law resides?"

"Ah, well, my husband says I am impetuous and usually right. So, he will be taking the job offer at the Cordoba airplane facility and I'll settle us into a nice home as my first priority. I am so excited! Maybe Julietta will have a regular Friday night babysitting job as Albert and I get to know the city. Oh, truly I hope we will remain friends and share our new beginnings!"

Papa spoke for all of us, "You will definitely hear from us and can expect a place at our dinner table. Lasagna with *bolognese* sauce and fresh green *insalata* on the menu as soon as we are settled." He sure could put on a good show, my Papa. Only we knew he was up to something!

THIRTEEN

❖

September 18, 1947

THE PORT OF FAIR WINDS

AND GOOD AIRS

The enormity of the M.S. Vulcania and its sleek design, novel diesel engine stacks, and magnificent splendor evoked whistles and cheers from crowds waiting at the port, as foghorns announced its arrival while it cut through the dense morning fog. Amazement and awe were an understatement, as very few luxury ocean liners had arrived at this port prior to our arrival. This simply wasn't an elegant port to arrive at, unlike our departure city of Genoa. Buenos Aires was founded as a port city in 1580, comprised of shallow, swampy terrain, where the Rio Plata emptied into the sea.

Docks at Puerto Madero, as the port is called, are lined with grain warehouses, shipping and rail yards, oil refineries, and the 50-year-old Hotel de Immigrantes, which provided disembarkation services, medical attention, and help finding employment for newly arrived immigrants. Accommodation was provided free of charge by generous ethnic benevolent associations until arriving immigrants found employment.

The process of disembarkation began with a team of immigration officials boarding the newly arrived ship to check documents of passengers before they were allowed to disembark. Medical checks were carried out on board by a doctor, preventing Immigrants with contagious diseases or mental health problems to enter the country. The inspection of luggage took place in one of the disembarkation sheds set aside for this purpose. The Hotel de Immigrantes has four floors and there were four dormitories per floor, each with a capacity of 250 people, giving the hotel a total capacity of 4000 people. When they first arrived, immigrants were given a number with which they could enter and leave the hotel freely, giving them opportunity to begin to know the city. Lodging was provided free for five days but could be extended in case of illness or continued job search.

Interpreters were provided, talks scheduled to explain aspects of life in Argentina, and identity cards were prepared. This building provided the entrance to other buildings in the complex, including the hospital, and it was from here both administration of the complex and planning and management of immigration in the entire country were carried out. Equipped with the most advanced medical equipment of the day, the hospital attended to thousands who arrived, some with diseases usually connected with effects of a long sea voyage, poor food on board, and generally terrible hygiene.

We were told arriving immigrants would be woken very early by wardens, with breakfast consisting of coffee, yerba mate, and bread baked in the hotel's ovens. During the morning, women would occupy themselves with domestic tasks such as laundering clothes and care of children, while the men were in the employment office trying to find jobs.

During and after the Second World War, many Europeans fled to Argentina, escaping hunger and poverty of the post-war period. Argentina also received thousands of Germans, including the humanitarian businessman Oskar Schindler and his wife. Also seeking a new homeland were hundreds of Ashkenazi Jews, and, for very different reasons, hundreds of Nazi war criminals. Notorious beneficiaries of European "ratlines" as they came to be called, included Adolf Eichmann, Josef Mengele, Erich Priebke, Rodolfo Freude (who became the first director of Argentine State Intelligence), and the Ustaše Head of State of Croatia, Ante Pavelić. It is almost unquestionably certain President Juan Perón was aware of their presence, and even invited these criminals on Argentine soil; consequently, Argentina was considered a Nazi haven for decades.

As the fog lifted, my family stood together on deck enjoying the morning sunshine and southern hemisphere warmth of early spring, during the chaos and commotion of disembarkation from the ship. Zio Paolo would not arrive until the following morning to retrieve us, and he had already informed us he would not be driving us through the very modern, Europeanized city at which we arrived. So, following advice and printed maps provided by of greeters at Hotel de Immigrantes, we headed out on a tour bus (with a bagged lunch they also provided) for as much sightseeing as we could manage with the few hours we had left after customs and orientation.

The first thing we noticed was the noise level created by vehicles of all sizes scurrying about the docks and on city streets. Soot and diesel fumes were heavy enough we coughed for several minutes after boarding the bus, and silently prayed it would clear up as we left the docks. Nico commented he hoped this wasn't representative of Latin American flavor, and we giggled while he coughed with exaggeration.

The tour bus was old and dingy, and its windows splattered with grime, but we found four seats together near the front where we could get the best views, while many other immigrants boarded. The driver called for everyone to be seated and pulled onto a large road, crossed railroad tracks and called out, "On this short bus tour, I, Martin de Avila Perez, will introduce you to Buenos Aires' most colorful neighborhoods which we call *barrios*. I will point out the greatest concentration of government buildings and the Presidential Palace, historic and memorable monuments and public squares, and very pricey exclusive homes in neighborhoods surrounding parks with names like Plaza Italia and the Parque Tres de Febrero. I'll call out their names and features with colorful stories about them, but I cannot answer questions, for you surely already notice all the honking and loud city noise, which prevents me from hearing you." He spoke Spanish, but his friendly tone and booming voice conveyed his message, and passengers quieted down so they could catch every word, mostly foreign to us.

Martin started the tour by taking us down Avenida de Libertador, through the Retiro with its art galleries and restaurants, many featuring Italian dining, both formal and cafe style venues. "Retiro was once known for being one of the wealthiest barrios in Buenos Aires. Casa de Retiro, meaning country retreat, was built by Governor Agustin de Roble at the beginning of the 18th century, but soon after, sold to the South Sea Company as home for the first slaves to arrive in the city. Here also, General Jose de San Martin gave orders to his grenadiers in a military barracks, repurposed from a bullring, to liberate the city from Engish invasion. Plaza San Martin with its equestrian statue honoring our great liberator is surrounded by our city's most impressive government buildings, and an opulent French-style palace, the grandest residence in Buenos Aires."

Peering outside the windows we were transfixed by the mix of modern buildings and wide avenues with buildings of Italian and French influence. Boulevards were lined with mature jacaranda trees, each with an amazing abundance of lilac flowers filling their thirty-foot crowns, draped over sidewalks filled with smartly dressed men and women, as you might see in Milan. Buenos Aires (good airs) in our new country of residence has been called "the Paris of South America", its most European capital city. I leaned over to Mamma and commented how she would look equally as elegant once she acquired some figure hugging outfits, surely sold in the elegant shops we were passing. Her reply was to lift one eyebrow and say, in a low sarcastic voice, "No doubt about that! It won't hurt for you to study these fashions so you can accompany me and we can both become stylish, right?"

Papa was listening intently to Martin, but I could tell he needed his favorite translator, so I would lean into him and whisper what I hoped was a reasonable translation. He is so quick to catch onto anything that captures his interest, but he has not had nearly the time and opportunities to learn this new language as the rest of us. I focused my camera for some photos as the driver stopped before turning onto Avenida 9 de Julio, the main boulevard, 16 lanes wide. We stopped in front of opulent Teatro Colon, "the city's most prominent landmark, a world-class forum for opera, ballet and classical performances. All of you must visit it and maybe some of you will be performers on its splendid stage!" remarked Martin, drawing oohs and aahs as he announced the buildings were influenced by French Renaissance, Beaux-Arts, and neo-classical architecture, and we peered at the huge Congress building modeled after the U.S. Capitol Building in Washington, D.C. Heads turned as he told us of the 22 story Palacio Barolo, inspired by Dante's Divine Comedy, with its cantos and verses and its divided structure referencing hell, purgatory and heaven. Unbelievably there's a lighthouse at the top with a 360-degree view of the city. Mamma turned around to inform us we will definitely be spending time to further discover these when we return to this "fascinating city".

Next stop, down Avenida de Mayo, was Plaza de Mayo, site of most important historical events since Buenos Aires' founding in 1884. "I normally allow my passengers to explore this exquisite park surrounded by the Metropolitan Cathedral facing Casa Rosada, home of our President Peron and his beautiful wife, Evita. They draw huge cheering crowds whenever they address their beloved citizens from that very balcony", Martin said as he pointed up, almost lovingly. "But we do not have time in this visit. We still have many delights in store as we drive through Recoleta, the wealthiest district, before heading to Palermo which most people are drawn to for its European lifestyle and affordable living, dining and night life. I often hear comments about how Parisian it feels to see families out walking and fishing at the beautiful urban open spaces of Parque Tres de Febrero and Plaza Italia. We are now approaching Cementerio de la Recoleta, final resting place of all the grand personages, memorialized in mausoleums and crypts so ornate as to make even the dead dizzy!"

We dined on our packed lunch of meatloaf sandwiches, apples, and caramel cookies called alfajores, as our coach whisked us through Palermo and back down Av. 9 de Julio to San Telmo, the oldest barrio in Buenos Aires, dating to the 17th century when it was first home to dockworkers and brick-makers. Martin told us this area of the poorest was uplifted by the establishment of the Parish of San Pedro Gonzalez Telmo in 1806. San Telmo here is the patron saint of seafarers. In Italy, we claim St. James, brother of John, beloved of Jesus for that title!

Martin proceeded, "San Telmo attracted the well-to-do after installing lighting, sewers, running water and cobblestones, when many mansions and imposing homes were constructed. But a cholera epidemic in 1871 claimed over 10,000 lives, causing many residents to flee. Due to this, San Telmo became intensely multicultural as waves of European immigrants made it their home and a lively place to enjoy antique shopping, street foods, and Tango out on the streets. Stop there for a maté or a cerveza and watch street artists, vendors and shoppers interact unlike any other place in this grand city."

Our final leg of this tour took us through La Boca, once a gritty shipyard bustling with European immigrants. The proximity to the Richuelo River is the reason for its very existence. Martin told us the first Italian immigrants settled here, thus now it is a most colorful barrio, and it is declared here, tango is king! I was delighted by the colorful artist's street by the water, though how they dealt with the smells from that river, I can't fathom. Nico plugged his nose with his fingers, causing me to laugh so hard, I spit out my partly chewed apple and got "the look" from Mamma.

Our first day off the ship, while we were disappointed Zio Paolo was unable to get a car to pick us up at arrival, was the best ever, and I can't wait to process the film and send my pictures to family and friends back home. "Home," now has expanded new meanings for us that reach across a vast ocean connecting the old with the new.

FOURTEEN

THE SHAPE OF THINGS TO COME

A s my uncle drove us through Cordoba, he proudly called out landmarks, monuments, memorials, squares and names of barrios and avenidas. Nico, always alert to military references, commented on the many streets bearing names of men of importance. It was with shock we learned a major boulevard had been named for Julio Argentino Roca, whose infamy lay in ordering the massacre of indigenous people of Argentina's south, by numbers so great they would qualify as genocide. His renowned acts drove back the Chileans as well, who had tried to align with indigenous Araucarian people against Spanish ranchers brazenly claiming their land. All to protect wealthy European-Argentinean landowners of these *estancias* from retribution by the people they had chased off their own lands!

"Tio Paolo!" Nico used the Spanish form of 'uncle' in our new home country. "Why is Roca celebrated for killing so many of the country's first people he nearly annihilated them? What is honorable about something so horrible? We've witnessed Europe torn apart while so many nations fought to stop this kind of horror against the Jews by Hitler's intentional plan for a pure Aryan race."

Before Paolo could respond, Papa bitterly proceeded from Nico's outburst. "We've heard rumors Argentina's Perónist regime is complicit in bringing ships full of Nazis fleeing Germany with enormous wealth plundered from their Jewish victims. God Almighty! We've heard the Vatican and Argentine cardinals are assisting in this. These must be lies. Tell us there is not truth in these reports."

Mamma sat stunned, not anticipating this outburst on the first day of our family reunion. Paolo shouted, "*Stai zitto, uomo!*" Shut the fuck up, man! You don't mention this in any discussion or conversation! You'll be quickly disapproved of and shunned if you speak poorly of our first lady, Eva Perón. People of all economic classes sing her praises. She and General Juan Perón have support of the labor unions. President Juan Perón has made good on his promise to labor unionists for land, higher wages and social security. The Peróns have brought great prestige and prosperity to Argentina. We should be grateful and overlook some of their means."

"Paolo, you want me to hold my tongue? We come from Italy, you and I, where all of us openly inform, discuss, criticize. It's not our way to be held back from dealing with social injustice, especially at crisis levels. I want to know what is true here. I am outraged -- we all should be -- those cold-blooded murdering *bastardi* responsible for the European war are welcomed here! They are hiding out here, while we had to flee the calamity war against them has left our land and people. How? Where? Do the people know? Obviously, you close-mouthed traitor -- YOU know!"

Tio Paolo pulled the car over crazily, nearly hitting one of many stray dogs who roam all the neighborhoods, even walking directly into shops. The dog let out a shriek as Paolo turned on my Papa. "You are my younger brother and I will not ever hear such disrespectful talk from you again!"

Paolo continued, "Lies? Everyone lies! The politicians could never be elected if they did not tell everyone what they wanted to hear, in every loud convincing speech they give. They do whatever it takes to get elected. And the followers lie to themselves in their belief this or that official will do right by them." My uncle continued speaking less heatedly,

"You were willing to believe you could escape Fascism and its evil next level, Nazism. You were willing to believe the New World would be more democratic, huh? Perón is no Mussolini, but this *is* a military regime, sort of a dictatorship. We do not live under tyranny! Argentineans celebrate their national holiday on 25 May when Revolutionists deposed the Spanish Viceroy -- the great war against the Royalists. We are becoming more leftist, approaching democracy. You have so much to learn! Come on, let's get on with our journey and you'll figure it out."

I was frightened and confused but I saw my father just turn away with disgust. What was on his mind? Could their opposing views be reconciled? The fact information isn't true doesn't matter when it's about ideology, not about truth. I already held the conviction I would never again live under tyranny with all its lies and misuse of the very people who placed trust in cunning despots. Mamma held my arm tightly, assuring me she felt the same.

Steering the car back into traffic, Tio brought us to our first Saturday night dinner with the Paolo Migliore family in their aging red brick home. The dinner table was being set with wine served to all at nine pm. Each of us was hugged and welcomed by my Tia Tina and cousins Silvia, Christiana, Anna and Matteo. We gave air kisses to the side of the cheeks and chatter began. There was all that looking each other over, and I found myself relieved Christiana, nearest my age, almost looked like me. She is seven years younger than her brother Matteo and almost eleven years younger than their sister Silvia.

I thought back to Mamma and Papa telling us all they could about them, and I laughed a little inside to recall

Christiana was an unexpected addition to the family. They all adored her despite adjustments it takes to bring a baby into a family so set in their routines. And then to be followed by little Anna with her auburn hair, masses of irrepressible curls restrained by a blue velvet hairband. Anna was only six when her family joined their papa in Argentina but has clung to the memories of her native land in war, all she can remember about Italy.

Dinner was amazing -- they had prepared a roast of the most tender and tasty beef I have ever had. That, surrounded by vegetables and potatoes served with gravy and salad, was all more sumptuous than almost any I had eaten since before war began in 1940. Warmth and wonderful smells from a familiar Italian kitchen, along with the comfort of being here at last, kept me from choking up with emotional overload. We set about eating and talking for hours following the incredible cannoli with pistachios made by my precious "new" family.

I began a study of every gesture and conversation of an immigrant Italian-Argentinean family. Being only slightly aware they were likewise studying our war-weary family, I was confident at least in our mutual love for *familia, patria* and *libertad*. There'd be a multitude of surprises in store for us which would take chapters of far too many impressions to write down, so I began by taking family photographs of every one of them and each one of us. By the end of that week, I had photographed our new home and neighborhood, our school (we wore school uniforms that made us look, well, uniform), the arrival of neighbors bringing casseroles to welcome us, and even the *panaderia* and butcher shop we would frequent daily. Nonno and Nonna would be thrilled once the rolls of film were developed and sent by ship. I hoped they would share them with Ani and Lorena, and it wouldn't take too long for them to arrive!

I made a mental list of topics of which I had much to learn, starting with my photographs and writing. I would have so much to share: school experiences, learning to speak, read, think and write in a new language, expanded shopping and markets for new foods and cooking, an entire new city and its barrios, transportation and safe or unsafe places, and varied climates (weather, cultural and political). Being very impressionable and almost totally unfamiliar with living in a large city, I welcomed the exceptionally loving preparation that Tia Tina and the family had in store for us. "*Dio mio,*" Matteo exclaimed. "We recalled what it had been like for us to be foreigners fleeing the European war. We wanted your arrival to be less a 'culture shock' and more a thrilling entry into an exciting new homeland for you to embrace." With that warmth I had to admit Papa may have made the best choice for him and his family!

There were no extra beds or bedrooms, but comfortable bedding was brought out for Papa and Mamma to sleep on the sofas, while I slept between Christiana and Anna, and Nico slept with Matteo. Talking and giggles from our room couldn't keep me from falling asleep. After all, the past two nights in Buenos Aires we had slept in what seemed like army cots in the Hotel for Immigrants. The warm welcome and service to us by strangers providing arriving immigrants good meals, translation assistance and health assessments at the entry point of this beautiful city are hallmarks of Italian inclusiveness and love. It was there I learned the Italians' history of immigration into Argentina, begun in the 1800's, was probably a greater consequence to South America, Brazil and Uruguay than their immigration to the

U.S.A. Italians had a choice between emigrating north to the United States or south to Argentina which, with considerable available land in the temperate zone, resembled parts of Italy.

After the War's end, Italy, reduced to rubble, occupied by foreign armies and choked with huge debt, saw a massive wave of Italians emigrating to South America. Their integration into Argentinean culture is shown markedly in faces of people with whom they have blended and had generations of children. It is manifested so clearly in neighborhoods and building styles, in the inventiveness and diverse talents, and even in *lunfardo*, the blending of words, as I was already beginning to notice.

FIFTEEN

October 1947

COUSINS AND STRANGERS

I live here in Argentina, my mind told my heart. My heart is really glad for it! I live here amongst *Cordobese Italianos* in an immigrant barrio with multi-generational southern Italian ways I recognize in these otherwise unfamiliar surroundings. Every day I help Mamma improve her Spanish as I seem to have picked it up fastest. These last weeks since arriving in the "New World" I hadn't had more than minutes to myself as I seem to be needed for every aspect of the move... to learn the language, streets, places, and dangers; I had to do my part to help make a functional household.

Tia Tina placed a hand painted sign above the front door of our home saying, "*Bienvenidos a Mi Casa*" and a rag rug at the entry to wipe off ever-present mud from our shoes before removing them. Mamma mentioned she would like to add *"Benvenuto e benedizioni a tutti che entrano."* Of course, with her beautiful, welcoming and generous spirit my Mamma would add the blessings, "welcome" to all guests who enter, in two languages! She got Nico to paint that greeting just below Tia Tina's.

Since Argentina has the opposite season to Europe, it was early spring here in October. Mamma and I shivered while removing our soaked jackets and gathered around the kerosene heater in the living room. Mamma fired up the pellet oven to warm the kitchen and bake the afternoon roasted meat. Papa had brought home a trussed pork roast last night so we could cook it today, and have leftovers for other meal preparations, like shredding and cooking it inside of a flat corn crepe called a tortilla. This enchilada meal was succulent when smothered with salsa made with tomatillos sauteed with onions, green chiles and lime juice, and served with fresh avocado.

Nico and Papa would arrive about one p.m. for the two-hour midday rest period we shared, until school started for Nico and me the following week. Since we lived so close to Tio Paolo, he was their driver. Their workday often ended at eight pm but they could sometimes get away earlier, holding a favored position at the meat packing plant as skilled butchers and management.

There had not been any antagonistic discussions recently. Except today when my Papa began his first week as assistant supervisor of the cut and pack division. Entering together, there was obviously huge annoyance between these two siblings and my impression was Papa was being browbeaten by his older brother.

Tio Paolo is so outspoken -- *schietto*! Against my Papa's manneredness and Mamma's polite restraint, his brashness --*brusco* -- was like a sudden clanging bell. I heard him say "Carmine, get sharper! There's no place in your current life here for making allowances for slackers. Someone's not performing to par, you must axe him. You'll appear the better for it; you'll get *per farsi notare en positivo*"

"I'm positively noticed already for excellence I bring to cutting meats," Papa replied confidently.

Paolo snorted lightly and continued, "And you'll still be passed over when time comes for bigger roles, bonuses and perks because you are not representing yourself assertively. You, you are the superior! You must have shown necessary toughness on men fighting under your command in the zone, eh?"

Papa laughed then and shook his head. "Paolo, you've been watching too many war movies. Resistance fighters lazy? Your brain is full of shit!" Still laughing he resumed, "For us, the battles were no game, no job, and certainly not judged by business standards. We gave all, every day and would do it again. Or maybe not, eh? To think Perón admired that fucking, lying Mussolini. He considered *Il Duce* to be Italy's greatest statesman of the century. Bah!"

Nico had been on a telephone call and we turned as he hastened into the living room in a disturbed state. "Donatello, Tulio and Marcus, the trio who unload carcasses from arriving trucks have been rounded up and taken into custody with no explanations given to the plant supervisor! He is looking for you, Uncle Paolo and you, Papa to help free them and meanwhile find at least three workers who can handle their work for the immediate future.

Paolo called and spoke to that supervisor who said he'd been frantically trying to gather the facts of this morning's events and to petition for release of these three young union members. "Tulio's brother had recently been fired from his post at the university for left-leaning and treasonous statements against Perón and has since been unable to find any work. Tulio, Donatello and Marco were identified by police as having been radical participants in demonstrations at the university. It seems that's enough to be forcibly arrested with no explanations and detained with no information as to the offenders' whereabouts."

Papa was standing alongside Paolo, the consternation on his face as serious as I had seen when he was a resistance fighter in Italy. "Paolo I can shuffle some competent workers to fill in for the three taken and I will notify their families." Paolo asked the supervisor for more details and learned three federal policemen had cuffed the workers and shoved them forcefully into a green sedan. He had seen Marco cry out as one of the officers billy-clubbed his shoulder, from which his arm seemed to hang. It was a frightful ordeal witnessed by himself and dozens of laborers at the plant.

Paolo became quite agitated at this news, cussing the police actions and even the Labor Relations Board and undercover informants, all of whom he said needed to be reported to President Perón. It was Nico who quieted him by saying Paolo needed to see the bigger picture and recognize these actions, proliferating every week, would never be tolerated unless the directive came from President Perón himself. I suspected had Papa mentioned this, Tio Paolo would have made a disgruntled retort to him. But while Nico continued, I was surprised to see Tio Paolo lower his head and say, "None of this makes sense. Yet, if what you are reporting is true, President Perón must have authorized crackdowns on protests. It sounds like he's targeting suspected dissidents expressing political sentiments he will not tolerate. I hadn't realized the extent of this infamy! Keep me informed of all you hear, Nico. And Carmine, thank you for taking quick action, and for not calling me out on the dense fog I have been walking in so confidently, even arrogantly"

Awkwardly I entered the room, hugged my Tio Paolo, super-hugged my Papa, and shrugged at Nico. "Now, lunch is on the table! Mamma is calling out, *mangia*!" Paolo left for his family meal and Papa took my hand with a wink in my direction.

And what does Paolo think of Nico? I once overheard him telling Papa it's just as well Nico is going to finish his high school studies since he's a daydreamer... "He needs a kick in the ass! And a girlfriend as smart as his mamma -- no mousy one!" Tio Paolo was never likely to appreciate Nico's inclinations towards art, architecture and leftist leaning politics. Still, I agree with Tio Paolo -- Nico just may need a kick in the ass!

When our working men return to their shifts at three, Mamma and I prepare for dinner, usually rushing out for our daily routine consisting of stopping at Piso's Panaderia for freshly baked crusty Italian loaves, sesame cookies and mezzaluna for breakfast. Next, we walk to Estancio's Verduria where we purchase salad (ensalada) ingredients: lettuce, tomatoes, celery and carrots (*la lechuga, los tomates, il sedano e los carotes* in my new language). Then over to Tia Tina's house for lessons in Spanish, Argentinean history and getting 'street smart'. I would be able to share photos from the voyage, our arrival, school and more, having already sent off the duplicates to our Nonni. Everyone scrambled to view and comment, providing great satisfaction to a budding belief in myself as a real photojournalist.

There's always such sweet sharing of Vietri and many family memories, especially when wine or limoncello gets poured -- in liqueur glasses for afternoons, of course. "Tina, those grapevines you and Paolo planted the year after you married in Vietri, they have been lusciously productive. I have at last seen the first new leaves on the scion which we brought from that vine and have planted on the arbor you can see from this kitchen window! Come look. I only wish we could grow citrus like we had back there! The arbor on which your original vine has grown all these years has been rebuilt already, and still frames the view over the town, focusing on "Two Brothers" emerging from the waters of the bay."

"Angelina, I so miss that life, the beauty of ancient roads leading to Villa Guariglia uphill and Chiesa della Madonna dell'Arco, that revered beautiful church from whose carved doors the road leads to the Amalfi coast. I adored the shops, invitingly situated in alleys guiding us into more remote corners of town, always accompanied by a citrus scent in the air. *Bellissima!*" Tia Tina gave words to the enchantment I read on her round face. Unlike most Argentineans who were slim, probably due to walking most places, and participating in sports and swimming, Tio Tina was plump. I expect blame could be placed on sampling the bounty of pastas and sweets she was famous for making.

"You're making me want to dance al rondo, Tina!" Mamma encouraged. Young Anna smiled with their recollections.

"Hey, I have a letter from Nonna to share about how much their garden yield has increased since neighbors have tripled their stock of chickens, enlarged the coop, and provided *molta merda di pollo* which makes super fertilizer! And Nonno mentioned he wishes to take a well-earned holiday to visit us all here during their winter, God willing!"

Mamma asked me to bring the letter over while she made cappuccinos for Tia Tina and steamed milk for cocoas for the girls. When I re-entered the room, I was carrying the letter and camera I employed for informal shots of a good time with *la mia famiglia Cordobese*!

Mamma has surpassed expectations of adapting to life in Argentina! Having lived for several years in Bologna where her papa was *professore* of International Studies and her mamma a tutor for some of his students in Italian language, Mamma and her three sisters and three brothers learned to be convincingly conversational in French and English. Her brothers learned German as well, but the girls finding it inelegant and harsh sounding, snubbed the students from Austria and Germany, except the few who chose to speak Italian with them. Nonna Militello often set the dinner table for up to a dozen, with little advance notice to their live-in housemaid. According to Mamma, "Her self-assured manner, inviting 'unfortunate students' living apart from their families, made us all comfortable with multi-culturalism and the vagaries of university life."

"Our home was lively and also lovely, blending Nonna's family heirlooms, precisely placed framed artworks (including creations of my siblings) and fresh flowers from the neighborhood open air market. She customarily included long stems of rosemary and borage from our garden in arrangements Nonno comically called her 'still life *al fresca*," Mamma mused one afternoon. Ominous black clouds and heavy gusting winds caused us to clip our ventures short and rush home following thunderclaps causing the dogs to cower.

"Hola, buongiorno!" Familiar voices called out from the foyer, using Spanish and Italian forms of hello, as Christiana and Anna stepped in from the storm. "We have

been knocking but assumed you might not hear us through thunder and pelting rain. Our mamma sent us over to bring these freshly harvested artichokes and brussels sprouts. Good thing she didn't come because we wound up running as fast as we could the last 3 blocks!"

Mamma rushed over with towels and chided we would have welcomed more rain in Southern Italy, so no negative comments on rain would be allowed here! My cousins removed their jackets, toweled their hair and faces and took the shopping bags towards the kitchen, while Mamma announced she had some bakery bought cookies and milk for them. We snickered when she commented, "I have less time than Tina to bake, since I began volunteering my nursing skills at the Italian Beneficial Society last week. They have warmly welcomed me, and I'm considering making lunch dates with new acquaintances. I hope you might know of some interesting places we can try out. I have already planned a lunch date with the wife of one of Tio Carmine's co-workers, at his encouragement."

"Before you knocked, Mamma had been reaching back to her memories prior to the fatal fire; she seems to have forgotten to mention her upcoming plans with me!" I chided her, feigned a look of hurt for the benefit of my cousins and added, "Now we know who counts" bringing friendly laughter all around.

"Tia Angelina, you are so much fun. I suppose you are adventuresome enough to try other than Italian cooking, so I'll tell you of some really good luncheon restaurants outside of our barrio, of course chosen to respect the budget of barrio dwellers! Christiana spoke in her assured manner. "In order of my favorites, there's always Mercado Norte where we frequent for meats of all kinds and empanadas, seafood and pizza -- you already know. Then there's the Parrillas, like Parrilla de Raul where steaks and mixed grills are amongst the best in all of Cordoba. You could go for Middle Eastern kabobs in Nueva Cordoba abundant in good eateries and outdoor seating -- so chic! My favorite is a small elegant Peruvian restaurant, family-run and so authentic! I'll get the name of it from my friend Vera, whose Tia and Tio own it. Maybe sometime *we* can have a girls' day out and lunch together -- would you, Tia Angelina?"

"You don't have to say please to that, and I proclaim Amen, my dearest ones! Even better, join me in an afternoon of volunteering at the I.B.S. and I'll treat you to dessert as well -- as long as they have chocolate fudge!" Lots of hugs ensued and a date for the girls' volunteering and lunch was set for Monday.

When they left, Mamma shared her plan to ask Valeria, the wife of Phillip, one of Papa's co-workers, recent immigrants from an Austrian mountain village to lunch. "Papa learned they have five children, the eldest two from Phillip's first marriage to Valeria's sister. When she passed away giving birth to her second child, Phillip wed sixteen-year-old Valeria. Imagine! She became an instant mother to her nephew and niece and three more have been born to them since. They have kept her house-bound and unable to make friends here. She speaks halting Spanish like I speak German, miserably. But it's a start. We're good at making starts, as you know!"

SIXTEEN

December 1947

FATEFUL CONVERSATIONS

VALERIA

Nearly a week ago, my husband, Phillip handed me a note from his supervisor Carmine's wife, Angelina inviting me to join her for a lunch so "two immigrants with husbands in the same meat packing plant could have a ladies' day out." I hadn't realized Angelina was so well versed in the dining spots in Cordoba when I agreed we could meet soon for lunch. But then, I ought to have expected she would prefer to try other than Italian fare, so her suggestion for Peruvian food, while outlandish, was tasteful in many respects.

Lunchtime at Maya's Andean Restaurant near the University district was packed with workers and students, but Lina (as she asked me to call her) arrived early and saved a small table with window view of a very busy shopping street and huge acacia tree directly outside. The menu, written on a chalk board, offered stews I was completely unfamiliar with. Drinks were also nearly incomprehensible, but I allowed my new, adventurous friend to guide me. What a treat we were in for, as the food was brought out in small portions for sharing ... goat stew made with yams, okra and a form of celery; tomatoes filled with bulghur and herbs, baked in clay pots and served with tiny breads of unknown origin. Lina grimaced while tasting lentils with breadcrumb and sour cheese topping. I could barely swallow the cow tongue barbequed over an open pit.

I wanted to know so much about this slim and lovely Italian immigrant whose husband worked with mine in the meat plant. Carmine and my husband Phillip have been sharing lunch breaks for nearly three months, but for Carmine's wife Angelina to suggest she would like to meet me was one of the sweetest gestures. I had only emigrated to Cordoba a few months before their family arrived, but I had not been welcomed by anyone prior to this. How can I engage in a conversation with someone who is probably not much more proficient in Spanish than I am?

I began, "Your husband has been the kindest friend to my husband, and now I have the chance to befriend you. In my native Tyrolean German we say *'So viel Gluck'*!" She sweetly responded, "In Italian, I say "*Tanta fortuna*!" and paused before adding, "In our newly adopted country it would be *'Tanta suerte*," and I broke into a smile, shyly hiding my crooked front teeth. More comfortable then, I asked her to tell me about her children. She humorously said that her two, Salvatore and Julietta, could probably be as boisterous as my five, and then asked me to tell her about myself and my children.

I rehearsed a response to this expected query with my 10-year-old son, who has attained such proficiency in Spanish he has earned top grades in this new language and in all his studies. With pride, I mentioned this about Alex and then counted off the younger ones who he was at home watching. "Claudia was born only one year after Alex, but she doesn't socialize well and is not as much interested in her studies. She adores playing the neighborhood gangs' untamed games of soccer and I love bringing the other children to watch her skills. So, then there is six-year-old Donnie who is my fair-haired and bold boy, followed by his two sisters, three-year-old Diana Louise and my *bebita*, eleven-month-old Martina, named for my mother who died of typhus during the war."

"Our village hid many Italian Jews fleeing Nazi Germans and Italian Fascists, who had remained loyal to the occupying force. Some of those we hid managed to escape from a train bound to a prison camp. Being a border community, we had German and Italian roots, so I understood the language of the Italian Partisan fighters. Some carried lice we washed them free from, but we could not eliminate typhus which caused a horrible outbreak amongst many whom I held dear. But that's war, isn't it?"

"I should know something about that, Valeria. As a Red Cross nurse volunteer, I knew of no families who had not suffered major losses. I try not to recall them, but the suffering and grief, while diminished, remain. My own bout with typhus caused me to miscarry twins and left me unable to conceive. Carmine still suffers from the grenade injury which ripped apart his left leg. I thank God every day his best friend carried him off the battlefield to a medic who drove like a maniac through enemy fire to bring him to a field hospital and then a fine Catholic hospital in Salerno. Typhus, malaria, diarrhea, even plague ravaged populations of fighting men and civilians, all more susceptible due to lack of nutrition, medical supplies and any semblance of sanitary conditions. As you said, that's war!"

"Angelina, most of my family has remained in our village, their home. I feel pangs of loneliness and I cry frequently. With my young children and my poor knowledge of the Spanish language and Argentine customs, along with my lack of education and skills, I'm so isolated. You're the first lady to befriend me, and I'm eager to have our families meet. How about a picnic next week when schools are closed in remembrance of some patriot's anniversary of liberation?"

"I'd welcome that, so we'll call it a date. My daughter Julietta loves children. I'm sure she will volunteer some childcare to free you up and get you out of the house sometimes? Anyway, I make a great lasagna good cold or hot, and Julietta is always up for baking cupcakes."

"My husband makes the most delicious sausage, which I'll bring with some snacks and iced tea, and we'll have an adventure. Minus the husbands, of course! Before you leave, Lina, I have an embarrassing request, so forgive me, but should you come across children's clothing which might be useful to my family, I would appreciate the consideration for our use. The children, they grow so fast, and we brought so little with us when we got on the boat -- third class of course, so even socks and shoes -- well, you know."

Angelina replied there's no shame in asking for some assistance and she'd do what she could to provide clothing for them. To myself I spoke these thoughts, "Here is an angel of mercy and kindness! Why then do I feel concerned for her safety? An immigrant herself, she helps the newer and downtrodden immigrants. Yet my husband has been told by our very own pastor he should maybe keep an eye on Carmine and his family. He claims they are refugees, immigrating here for political asylum and may be Communists. I don't know why? I just know I won't have her come to harm. I just want to get to know her better, and if I should be telling my husband about what she and Carmine do, God help me, I might not tell him all."

Angelina must have noticed me withdrawing inside my head, as she spoke, "Valeria, tell me about your husband and where you have immigrated from.

"Phillip is a decent, hard-working man with a huge appetite for things in life to be passionate about," I laughed as I spoke. "He'd been married to my oldest sister until she died giving birth to Claudia, being so undernourished from the impossibility of having adequate food during those times. So, Phillip asked me to be his bride. We love bringing all five children up together, but he is of little help, and I get so tired! I guess he is like many Italian men, who I hear come home from work, expect dinner on the table, and must have a beer or three. Then he usually burps and coughs and cusses before dozing in his easy chair. I get the children bathed, read them a good night story and kiss their sweet foreheads each night, then sneak off for a few minutes of peace with some vin santo before shaking him to get into bed. Most nights he is frisky and rough with me, but the church says our bodies belong to our husbands, so we must submit. I just hope we don't have any more babies. Really, I do! Maybe I have said too much?"

Seeing the consternation on Angelina's face, I shut up quickly and lowered my eyes. My education was only through seventh grade, but I recognize when I've put my foot in my mouth, or if I've revealed too much. "I'm not meaning to complain. Phillip respects Carmine and Paolo and these words should not be shared, but I feel so overlooked and fatigued sometimes I wonder if the prayers and the solace of the pastor will be enough to carry me through."

While babbling on, I noticed there were patrons waiting for a table. Suggesting we give up our seat and pay for lunch helped me overcome the awkwardness which my exposé caused. There wasn't much more to say until we walked out to the bus stop. Lina touched my shoulder, then linked her arm in mine and said, "Listen, Valeria, you are made in the image of God. That is what your pastor should be telling you and advising your husband. You're the loving support of him only insofar as he is kind to you. That is *his* duty! Understand you deserve protection, love, help and support from your husband, not expect to be an object in his household to manage after him and his children. What kind of priest advises a wife to put up or shut up? He doesn't sound like a man of God."

I was shocked and dismayed. If I cannot trust my priest, what then? "Angelina, I cannot speak these things to my husband. He has hit me for being a 'mouthy bitch' and I have no skills to fall back on if he throws me out!" Now I knew I had gone too far, so I smiled and pointed to the upcoming bus and said I must be on that bus. She smiled back at me and handed me the note she had scribbled while I was talking. It read, "Picnic lunch Friday 11:30 at the pavilion next to the south shore of the lake in Sarmiento Park. Angelina 351-434-3536."

Aboard the bus I thought back on what I had told her. While I was supposed to be learning information about her and activities her family might be involved in, I couldn't keep my own mouth shut long enough to learn anything. Padre Russell may need to feed me questions so I could better find out if Angelina's family has communist leanings and whatever else he insists I learn about them. I just don't know if I'm up to it. Passing the *biglietto* to the conductor, I shoved one hand into a pocket, with the handle of my purse held firmly next to my body and used my left hand to hold the ring above the aisle to keep my balance while the bus swayed. I sensed some queasiness, possibly nausea and hoped to God it was only swaying of the fast-moving bus. In my head I counted back to when I last had my period -- 5 weeks. Please, God, let that be merely a side effect of nursing my *bebita*, please!

What was it Padre Russell last confided to Phillip and me? My brain is still processing today's luncheon conversation with a new friend, as I fight to recall what our priest asked of me. Vaguely I conjured up his request I visit

Angelina at home and share my love for Christ at their traditional home altar, where she surely would have an Infant of Prague. He expressly mentioned that Infant of Prague, but I doubt he had ever been invited to their house. Oh, I have too much to be concerned with and must follow what I'm told to do or risk displeasing Padre and my husband. Yes, that's what I will do.

SEVENTEEN

December 1947

NEW SCHOOL, NEW FRIENDS, NEW TRUTHS

O ddly, the school I now attend is not so physically different from the one I left in Vietri, except instead of the omnipresent religious portraits of Blessed Virgin, Jesus' Sacred Heart, the Holy Trinity and saints we all recognized (and many prayed to) there were pictures of President Juan Perón and his wife Evita. Adoration for her generous and immensely popular outpourings held forefront whenever "Saint of the Poor" Evita was spoken of, since there could be no unpleasant aspects of the Argentine first lady. After President Perón married Evita in the fall of 1945, she gave up her radio-star-turned-movie-star career to play a prominent role in the Perón social program, always pointing honors to her husband. Evita sponsored a law which brought equal rights to Argentine women, and she was a strong supporter of labor unions, softening whatever military predispositions *el Presidente* might otherwise be inclined. The blonde chignon, which became her signature style along with furs and jewels, crowned her head as a halo would a saint.

My 8th grade teacher, Señora Alvarez sat me next to Christiana in a trial to determine if my studies were equal to what my fellow students had been learning. In a short time, despite the limiting language barrier, it was determined I had sufficient educational background in nearly all subjects as the other students so I could continue at this grade level. Señora Alvarez was warm, funny and compassionate. She would close the doors on Friday afternoon and play music we could dance to in a very modern fashion. Living in Argentina was drastically different from my Italian roots and being shy wouldn't serve me, so I gladly joined in all social events, including the all-girls lunch table, and at recess playing dodge ball or jumping-rope activities.

There were at least a dozen immigrant students in eighth grade, none of them proficient in Spanish, so we took Saturday classes and together struggled. Frank Ernst was a very good-looking German boy who seemed to have a crush on me. I would blush when aware of his sharp blue eyes staring at me, offering a friendly invite to perhaps find out more about his interest. I liked his perfect smile, his non-arrogance towards other students less gifted than he, and his good-natured playfulness within our class circle. His Spanish being clumsy, he asked me to help him, arriving earlier for class and sharing an yerba maté. I looked directly at him, hoping he didn't notice my pleasure but his smile was reassuring and somewhat shy.

I welcomed spending more time with Frank greatly, but I dared say no more than yes. So began the unexpected friendship between what I could have assumed to be the son of a former Nazi and me, the daughter of a Pro-Allied Resistance Officer -- no suspicions, prejudices or judgments, not initially at least. Frank's presence next to me and our greater familiarity over the ensuing month of Saturday morning meetings, created a spark that emboldened me to suggest hanging out at school events, and eventually led to our meeting at the Friday night outdoor market near the canal and restaurants a few blocks from my home. The Italian neighborhood known as Barrio Guemes was similar to what I had seen in Naples with crowded brick row houses for families of laborers. There it is referred to as a ghetto; here, you will not find trash strewn about, but rather brooms at each doorway to sweep clean steps and sidewalks. In both cities you would also find grannies missing teeth and wearing aprons over their large bosoms. Nonni could be seen at the markets, on buses and in clinics caring for as many as four or five grandchildren, to allow their own children to hold jobs. Unlike in Naples, people here never seemed burdened, but rather, more full of heart.

I had to know my new friend better before having him meet my family, probably beginning with Christiana and my brother. By our third mate´ and tutoring session, Frank asked me to stay after class to meet his parents who were walking to school to pick him up and spend the rest of the day helping out at the German Mutual Aid Society. What harm could come of just saying a polite hello and heading off shortly to meet up with my cousins. I knew they'd be waiting at the corner drugstore
for all the details.

"Should I call your parents Dr. and Mrs. Ernst?" I asked.

"Sure, why not? My father specializes in diseases of eye, ear, nose and throat. His practice is downtown near the Court of Justice where all the lawyers can be found. So I tease, with his sharp vision, he always seems to be inspecting me and I joke the barristers are equally as myopic as he!"

"But my mother has a specialty of her own. She is a master gemologist. Her German Jewish grandparents began a custom gem and gold business in Berlin which stayed in the family until the night of 9 November 1938 known as *Krystallnacht*. There's not enough time now to tell you more about that, but my parents and grandparents fortunately escaped Nazi Germany, having lost so much. Once their shop's windows were smashed and everything not locked away looted, they fled with their lives, some savings, and their remarkable skills into Belgium." Frank revealed this just before the handsome couple, his parents approached us, leaving no time to digest it all.

Dr. and Mrs. Ernst were, as I expected, quite well dressed in tailored overcoats and very fine shoes. I had hoped to glimpse some marvelous jewelry on their necks and fingers, but aside from matching gold rings and simple but surely expensive gold watches, there was only a starburst brooch on the scarf worn by Mrs. Ernst. How different from the Italian mothers who had pierced earlobes and gold earrings, either filigreed or with a pearl, sapphire or diamond, hanging as a pendant from a gold hook. Frank must have prepared them for me as they showed no surprise at my nearly 5'8" height, fully an inch taller than Frank and his father.

Frank, always outgoing and confident, led me to his parents with his arm at my waist, so comfortably, I quickly relaxed. "Father and mother, I present Julietta Migliore, the brightest girl in my class, and an immigrant from Vietri sul Mare in Southern Italy, for only three months now!"

Dr. Ernst nodded and simply said "Hello, and Welcome!" Mrs. Ernst warmly took my hand in both of hers and welcomed me with "It's my pleasure to meet the girl Frank holds in such high esteem." Her smile elicited from me a warm easy smile in return. Frank commented, "Smiles like those break down culture barriers. I already feel like we have more in common than most other students in our class."

Dr. Ernst then suggested we should set a "date" for brunch on Saturday at Novecento Ristorante, near the Iglesia Catedral. "You should find it easy to arrive by bus from Guemes to Plaza San Martin where we can meet you and walk together to the café, a special find we enjoy for its mellow comfort. Not pretentious, just stylish enough, and the food is always excellent."

Frank intoned, "My command of Spanish is wanting, but my parents are quite fluent enough to fill in my uncomfortable voids. Your Spanish is good, Julietta, so I expect we'll both benefit from conversing, plus we love introducing friends to foods and places we love."

I needed no convincing, so readily agreed to the plan and mentioned to Mrs. Ernst I was fascinated to learn as much as I could about her work and background in gemology. Mrs. Ernst offered to show me photos she had taken of her unique jewelry creations and some rare acquisitions in her collection. She had international buyers, so had learned to take professional photos with her Leica and was proficient in Spanish, French and English to facilitate commerce.

In awe, I stammered I could hardly wait, and Mrs. Ernst proposed she, Frank and I should meet the next afternoon at the bookstore down one block from school. Everyone knew this enormous bookstore with its reading room, café, and late hours open until midnight!

"I will be there with Frank right after school, and with your permission, would like to bring my own Leica camera and some select photos I have taken. It would mean the world to me if you would teach me beyond basics and nuances of photography."

"I'm sure I can and I'm eager to help you explore multiple avenues of photography. My father passed on his Leica to me, having used it from macro-photographs of every piece of jewelry which passed through our shop, to landscape photographs of architectural and natural wonders, many of which were destroyed in the war. I proved an able learner and am open to learning more sophisticated techniques, maybe together?" Mrs. Ernst remarked, and then was hurried off by Dr. Ernst and Frank to their assignment at the German Mutual Aid Society.

Nico was on the bus I boarded for home and remarked on seeing me with three strangers at the stop. "So, my sister is meeting up with unknowns after school! Would you have told me about them if I hadn't seen them?" he chided. He, of course, was surrounded by some fairly rowdy high school students and one of the boys leaned in asking to be introduced to the new girl. Taking that cue, I asked as well to be introduced to the new girl sitting next to Nico.

"My sister Julietta, an eighth grader, usually takes the earlier bus with our cousins. Ricardo, Chachio, and Luca are my *compadres* in radicalism. We hold regular study groups focused on historical and political movements and I've invited these three over to our house for a meeting this afternoon. Luca's father has been fitting out a space to serve as a clandestine meeting room at the back of his bookstore, named for her, for private study groups."

"My God, I am so interested -- I mean, if I could be included?" I blurted out as several students pushed their way past me, knocking my bookbag to the filthy floor of the bus. "*Que tan grosero es eso?* I shouted over to them, upset over how rude they were. Ricardo helped retrieve my bag and said, "Glad to give you a hand, *senorita!*"

"*Gracias*, Ricardo" remarked the youngest in the group, me! In the space of one afternoon, I received attention from two attractive boys, and I saw Nico wink as I reddened. He shouted out, "Next stop is ours." Luca walked out followed closely by Nico, then Chachio and Ricardo who flanked me asking about my school and interests.

"Photography, writing, history and nature are my loves. Oh, and cooking -- I love Italian dishes, but my new favorites are Argentinean empanadas and meat stews. If you are staying for dinner, I have made a *Carbonada Criola* we serve over homemade noodles. Along with Italian bread dipped in olive oil, we should have enough for all of us." I said as they made slurpy sounds.

"Maybe a taste, Nico suggested, as they have their own dinners planned with their families, right?"

"You must be loco, *mi amigo*! My stomach is growling, my mouth is watering, and I wouldn't dishonor the senorita by turning away her home cooked meal!" Ricardo stated and Chachio agreed. Luca just laughed and we arrived home.

Mamma had not yet returned from assisting more recently arrived Italian immigrants. I appreciated they were so fortunate to have her services, so I filled the void by setting out some sliced salami, roast beef and provolone cheese on a ceramic platter we found at the barrio's Friday night flea market last week. I handed Nico a cutting board, knife and loaf of crusty bread and asked for volunteers to set out dishes and serve refreshments. Ricardo flicked Matteo's arm to show he was more than eager to lend me a hand. Luca nibbled some bread and cheese as Nico served them and then headed into the kitchen to offer assistance. I had been heating the *Carbonada* and set water to boil for the noodles. While turning to get a good look at Luca, I handed her the plates to set out on the table and asked some of the many questions popping up.

"*Bienvenido*, would be my Mamma's greeting so I will extend that to you! Do you take many classes with Nico? Has he told you much about us -- our family, I mean?"

Luca had a beautiful smile, a glow which emanated through her pores, her eyes, her wavy blonde hair. *She* would never need to be assertive, as she had a magnetism neither forced nor subdued. It just drew one towards her as you'd be drawn to a calmly observing baby. She spoke, "I feel so glad to meet you and soon your Mamma, since I can then confirm the delightful things Nico has spoken about the women in his life. I share three classes with him -- World Civilization, Chemistry, and Math. We started studying difficult algebraic and trigonometric functions together and a bond emerged. You see, besides our school studies, we both have hearts afire over communist principles and social activism. I'm not giving away too much, I hope?"

I chuckled, "Not to another kindred activist in the making, which I am! Nico has spoken of you, frequently and as you must be aware, fondly. I'm glad to see you are not blushing, as I use no filters with friends and I've never learned to be coy," I replied truthfully. "My brother has spoken admiringly about the enterprise with your father so be prepared for us to barrage you with questions as we will want to get to know you better as well."

"Luca, you are the first Polish national I have met. You are also the first girl I've met who has expressed an interest in politics and foundations for a new civil order. My cousins probably think I am too radical and secretly suppose that Nico is a communist!"

While we both giggled over that, Mamma arrived, and we could hear Nico introducing them. "*Bienvenido*." greeted Mamma, "Can you stay for dinner?" she offered, which elicited "*Grazie*" from Matteo and "*Gracias*" from Ricardo. Then, noticing Luca she added, "This must be Luca! Well then, set three extra plates, Julietta."

Our dinners, like all Argentineans, were about nine pm. Mamma just left us to eat and later joined the table for maté and conversation.

"It seems you are all comfortable speaking Spanish so feel free to correct any of my incorrect word choices. First, are all of you immigrants? Share with me some memories of your country of departure and how you found yourself in Cordoba, *por favore*." Mamma drawled out the last phrase in Spanish.

"Matteo and I are immigrants, arriving five years ago on the same ship out of Spain, though he is from Bologna, Italy and I am from Barcelona! replied Ricardo. "My family of 2 sisters and 2 brothers was shuffled right out of Franco's Civil War dangers by my great aunt, who had immigrated to Cordoba in the 1930's. Aboard the ship, our dining room companions were the Romanello's, including Matteo, his four sisters and his charming, well-educated parents and godparents. My father talked so glowingly of all the opportunities and schools in Cordoba, Matteo's entire family decided, even before we disembarked in Buenos

Aires, they would follow us, their new friends, to experience a new life in Cordoba."

Matteo broke in, "Hey, let me tell some of my story! Bologna is the most beautiful city in the Emilia-Romagna and my family has lived there for over three hundred years! Once Italy returns to prosperity under Communist leadership, my family will prefer to return to our ancestral lands and to positions of professional chefs and productive estate owners. From the tower of our *castello piccolo* one can see the leaning tower -- of Bologna! That always brings laughs, but it is truth! Our small castle was nothing like is found in Florence, but in Bologna you can meet your fellow Bolognese citizens at the train station restaurant where they serve the best weekend brunches. Families show up there right after Synagogue or church services, dressed in fine clothes which never get stained as they swirl their pasta around the fork. Our meat sauce is not so thin that it drips, and it is made from local ingredients farmed in the richest soil Italy offers!"

Nico nearly choked with laughter as he broke in, "This same pride of our origins holds true for all of us gathered at our humble table, so enough of your boasting -- let's hear from my special girl, Luca."

"First, pass the cheese, Matteo, *grand uomo,* and an extra napkin as I'm not yet adept at swirling pasta around my fork without any spots landing on my blouse." Luca clearly knew these friends well to be tossing retorts like one of the boys, suggesting more reasons to want to emulate her. "Warsaw was deliberately annihilated in 1944 as a retaliatory act for Polish resistance to Nazi German occupation. Warsaw was the proud capitol of my home country Polonia. But I will never return to Poland, ever. My father, Walter, may still be a wanted man, and my mother and grandparents were victims of the ghetto wall bombings. I am now a citizen of Argentina and I speak two of its languages very well, Spanish and Italian!"

"Not to mention she is a good capitalist on the outside and a good revolutionary in her blood and guts. This, Mamma, is the co-owner with her father of the Nuevo Cordoba R.E.L.L.-- *Revolucion en Los Libros*, officially Luca's Bookstore. Soon we'll be having weekly clandestine meetings in their backroom, surrounded by books which are amazingly good at muffling sound and conversations and as Luca's father advised, are best to stop bullets. So, as long as we seem to be "regulars" or customers, we'll be safe."

"If that's meant to be reassuring, it has done nearly the opposite," Mamma replied. "I want to be kept fully informed, you understand! Consider me a source for reference, information, playing the devil's advocate and even, sometimes, attendance if am welcome."

There was unanimous agreement. Our first meeting was scheduled for one week from tonight, and the topic would be "What are the current conditions in the country which you have left." All eager to prepare for our part in this discussion, we would gladly have put off doing our homework, but Mamma vetoed that idea, saying we needed to be tops in our class before we could be students forging revolutionary ideas. Or at least concurrently.

EIGHTEEN

FORGOTTEN PAIN

I so wanted to be taught the real history of the 1900's. Surely this school in Cordoba would have a broader more scholarly scope of goings-on in Europe and the Americas which led to events culminating in two great world wars. Señora Alvarez announced she would be showing film strips featuring World War II: conditions leading up to the war, Allied Forces vs. Axis, the battles and the treaties. Our textbook reading assignment covered the years from 1938 to 1945 when Hitler and Nazism, Mussolini and Fascism, and Japan and Imperialism almost destroyed Western democracy. How strange it was just three chapters. Only three chapters!

Señora Alvarez began by showing us a newsreel, first of two BBC short documentaries on World War II: Fascism in Italy, followed the next day with a film about the history of Germany's 3rd Reich. "Students, once you have read the assigned chapters, and taken notes on the newsreels, I will call on each of you to write a report and will ask to have the most well written read aloud."

Respectfully, but knowing my face was overshadowed with shock, I asked Señora Alvarez, after the students had rushed out, how so little reading could be assigned about the most consequential event of the 20th century. Her eyes then pierced my own as she suggested I write a report to fill in the voids, beginning with an outline I should submit within the week. I titled it "World War II. The Deadliest War Could Have Been Avoided."

Standing at the front of the classroom, I began my report by acknowledging the presence at the back of the room was my Mamma. This report, itself, was thanks to her immense contributions as she had been educated in Bologna, where her father was a professor and head of the

Linguistics Department at the oldest university in Europe. It was at her suggestion I asked Señora Alvarez if I could write definitions for terms some students might find unfamiliar. She offered, "I'll do even better, Julietta. I will write them on the blackboard to remain until we have classroom discussions following both of your presentations! What must classroom visitors have wondered when they encountered: SUBVERSIVE; REPRESSIVE; BUNKER; ARMISTICE; UNCONDITIONAL SURRENDER.

Standing beside Señora Alvarez, facing the attentive class, I began with a statement Adolf Hitler made in his detestable book, Mein Kampf:

> *"The best way to take control over a people and control them utterly is to take a little of their freedom at a time, to erode rights by a thousand tiny and almost imperceptible reductions. In this way, the people will not see those rights and freedoms being removed until past the point at which these changes cannot be reversed."*

> *From his prison cell in 1925, he wrote: "The receptivity of the great masses is very limited, their intelligence is small, but their power of forgetting is enormous. In consequence, all effective propaganda must be limited to a very few points and must harp on these in slogans until the last member of the public understands what you want him to understand by your slogan."*

Standing in front of my peers who were eager to be better grounded in a more scholarly overview of the war we had lived through, I spoke, "Now we know Hitler took irreversible steps of removing the people's freedoms, while provoking them to detestable hostilities towards Jews. The Fuëhrer maniacally ranted and blasted lies supplied by his minister of propaganda, Josef Goebbels. This high-ranking Nazi's methods and media were designed to express Hitler's divine dominance over any people and nation. It's a fact once he had assumed full dictatorial powers through the Enabling Act of March 1933, opposition to Hitler amounted to high treason. All members of the armed forces had to swear the oath of allegiance, not to Germany, but to Hitler!"

"God has made me Fuëhrer and ruler of every man and woman of German blood in every country on earth!" Hitler boasted. Does anyone wonder he would not have carried out his designed plans for world domination -- a Third Reich for which God designated him leader -- without active cooperation of the German nation?" I paused and looked at my classmates who sat solemnly, some even nodding, and some with a puzzled look on their faces.

"We have seen photographs of bonfires throughout Germany when he ordered books to be banned and burned, claiming they were decadent and subversive. All civilized people recognize these acts are an abhorrent symptom of a repressive society. Meanwhile, in the name of the superiority of the Aryan race, he elevated German composers and authors who represented the noble German society. Let me read on:"

"All human culture, all the results of art, science and technology that we see before us today, are almost exclusively the creative product of the Aryans."

And now we know he intended to eradicate any 'inferior' race or culture. While the world looked on, he forced anyone with Jewish blood, all Gypsies, the mentally ill and disfigured, and anyone considered an enemy of the state into concentration camps. Senora Alvarez will shortly be showing a documentary newsreel, whose visuals and information you will see and hear provide adequate evidence of the horrors a totalitarian government with absolute dominion over its populace has done. If history does repeat itself, you can be certain that form of government will force its evil agenda on a willingly blindsided population again."

The Final Days, A Report by Julietta Migliore

The final days of the Nazi empire showed the depths of Hitler's capacity for self-delusion. Children and old men were mobilized in a desperate attempt to fill the decimated remains of the German army. As the Allies invaded from both east and west, Hitler refused to surrender, believing he could hold out. He refused to listen to advice of his commanders, who one by one deserted him. One of them, Guderian, a rare voice of reason, was sent away for repeatedly arguing with Hitler.

It was only as Berlin was falling to the Soviets, amidst the ruins of the nation wrecked by his unwillingness to face reality, in Hitler's final moments, he left these testimonials:

> *"Centuries may pass, but from the ruins of our cities and artistic monuments hatred will constantly be renewed against that people that must ultimately be held responsible for everything: international Jewry and its helpers!*
>
> *But I have also made it quite clear that, if the nations of Europe are again to be regarded as mere shares to be bought and sold by these international*

conspirators in the world of money and finance, then there is one people that will be held responsible, that is the real culprit in this murderous struggle: Jewry! I also left no one in doubt that this time not only would millions of the children of Europe's Aryan people die of hunger, not only would millions of adult men suffer death, and hundreds of thousands of women and children be burned and bombed in the towns, without the real criminal, albeit by more human means, having to atone for that guilt.

After six years of war which, in spite of all the setbacks, will go down in history as the most glorious and valiant demonstrations of a nation's life-will, I cannot abandon the city which is the capital of this Reich. As the forces are too small to make any further stand against the enemy attack at this place and as our resistance is gradually being weakened by men who are as deluded as they are lacking in initiative, by staying in this city I should like to share my fate with those, the millions of others, who have also assumed the task of doing so. Moreover, I do not wish to fall into the hands of an enemy who requires a new spectacle organized by the Jews for the amusement of their overheated masses.

I have therefore decided to stay in Berlin and, of my own free will, to choose death there at the moment when I believe that the position of Fuëhrer and Chancellor itself is no longer tenable.

I die with a happy heart, conscious of the immeasurable deeds and achievements of our soldiers at the front, of our women at home, the achievements of our farmers and workers and the work, unique in history, of our youth, who bear my name.

That I express my thanks to you all from the bottom of my heart is just as self-evident as my desire that you should, because of that, on no account give up the struggle, but rather continue it against the enemies of the Fatherland, no matter where, true to the creed of the great Clausewitz.

I demand of all Germans, all National Socialists, men, women, and all the men of the armed forces, that they be faithful and obedient unto death to the new government and its president.

I myself and my wife – in order to escape the disgrace of deposition of capitulation – choose death. It is our wish to be burned immediately on the spot where I have carried out the greatest part of my daily work in the course of twelve years' service to my people."

Signed A. Hitler

I felt a need to clarify further, "Carl von Clausewitz was a 19th century Prussian general and military theorist who stressed the "moral" (psychological) and political aspects of war. For example, he wrote, 'War is the continuation of politics by other means," and "If the leader is filled with high ambition and if he pursues his aims with audacity and strength of will, he will reach them in spite of all obstacles."

"Hitler correctly diagnosed the cowardice of Western European nations to enforce terms of the Versailles Treaty, and their appeasement efforts towards his blatant major rearmament and build-up of all Germany's armed forces. Isolationism and avoidance of conflict, the turtle shells covering nearly all non-Germanic nations following The Great War, World War I, allowed Hitler to achieve early successes, that quickly and terribly placed the fate of Europe in his hands. His goal was to reunite the German-speaking people whose land had been carved into independent countries by the Treaty of Versailles, through absorbing Austria, taking Czechoslovakia, then expanding to Poland, Belgium and France. Once Poland was invaded, France and England with their pledges of mutual support, both declared war on Germany. Mussolini's Fascist Italy played right into Hitler's schemes. Germany wanted to conquer Europe, Italy to dominate Africa and the Mediterranean and their third evil partner, Japan, wanted to rule over a New World Order in Asia. By 1940, Hitler controlled much of Western Europe. On December 7, 1941 Japan bombed the U.S. Naval Base at Pearl Harbor, Hawaii and the U.S. Congress declared war on Japan. Within days, Japan's allies, Germany and Italy, declared war on the United States."

I began the following day by returning to the consequences of Hitler's pure Aryan agenda. "Hitler left the testimonials I spoke of yesterday, and then he shot and killed himself rather than face the consequences. Ashes found in the bunker were not conclusively proven to be his, but then he insisted nothing could remain which could be defiled."

"A journalist wrote this in the May 14,1945 issue of Life Magazine, one of many issues which my Papa saved: "When the sun came over Germany on May 5, it was a wonder that it did not stand still... There was an image from Wagner's myths: a blazing room in the Reich Chancellery in Berlin, a pyre for a fake god who may or may not have been consumed in flames."

"In general, the League of Nations, composed of members from all continents, was supposed to safeguard the peace of Europe as part of world peace. Really? League of Nations? After six years of World War with its unfathomable destruction and two atomic bombs, crimes piled upon crimes and the Europe we knew collapsed, mankind can *only* be stunned, and in response, desire to lash out, be punitive, and then attempt to re-build. Can we establish an organization of nations to save the world from self-destruction?

My final statement to the class was, "I am certain that will not be the end of evil despotism, as long as tyranny is tolerated in any of its forms."

I posed Mamma and Señora Alvarez in front of the blackboard with the vocabulary words and took pictures of them. Frank came up beside me and motioned for me to get into the picture. "Julietta, I can competently handle a few photos with this camera. It is nearly identical to my Mutti, oops, mamma's"

Remarkably, I still have those photographs in my prized album. Papa suggested for the security of Señora Alvarez, I must be careful not to show them to anyone who might consider the Señora too liberal and not adequately Pro-Perón. I mentioned this to her, and she showed relief I would maintain confidentiality so she would not be at risk of losing her position. I was already aware President Juan Perón was an authoritarian head of a government which placed great loyalty amidst its propagandized media and institutions.

NINETEEN

IRON ARM, COLD HEART

Señora Alvarez had allowed me to present both of my reports. The entire class paid rapt attention as I spoke about the 'other dictator', Italy's own Benito Mussolini. "My Papa, as mentioned in my Hitler report, had saved several Italian newspaper headline pages and magazine articles that he insisted be ingrained in his memory and be published proof he could share with doubters. Papa helped me write this report on Mussolini, with raw emotions and extreme determination, to provide a full picture of, in Papa's words, this 'traitorous fool".

This excerpt from an interview with Benito Mussolini at Palazzo Monforte in Milan reveals the self-delusion successfully convincing to his Fascist followers:

"Let these stormy years pass. A young man will rise. A single-minded man. A leader who fully embodies the ideas of Fascism. Collaboration and not class struggle; charter of work and socialism; property sacred, as long as it does not encourage poverty; care and protection of workers particularly the old and invalids; care and protection of mother and child; fraternal support for the needy; morality in every field. Struggle against ignorance and submissiveness towards the powerful. In so far as there is still time, strengthening of self-rule, our single hope until this utopian day when there will be division of the raw materials that God has given to the world, among all nations; glorification of the pride in being Italian; education in depth and not only at the surface, as has unfortunately happened because of events and not because of ideological inadequacy."

"A single-minded young man will come, who will find our postulate of 1919 and the program of Verona of 1943, who will put them into action in a fresh, bold and worthy

way. The people's eyes will then be open, and the triumph of these ideas will be prepared. It was in too many people's interest for these ideas not to be understood and valued, and many believed that they infringed the moral and material interest of the people. We have lived through 18 centuries of invasions and misery, of falling birth rates, servitude, internal struggles and ignorance. Above all, however, centuries of poverty and malnourishment. Twenty years of Fascism and seventy years of independence have not been enough to give the soul of every Italian the strength to overcome the crisis and understand the truth. The great and numerous exceptions were not enough."

"These proclamations sounded like the hopes and dreams every Italian would realize under the founder and leader of Fascism. This is exactly the genius of tyrants to use such rhetoric with gestures of power and authority, causing the citizen masses to loudly proclaim him their leader, "il Duce."

"The Italian people have not overcome this crisis, which began in 1939. They will rise again, but the convalescence will be long and sad, and full of woe if there are setbacks. I am like the great clinician who has not succeeded in providing the correct treatment, and who has now lost the trust of the important patient's family. Many doctors are pushing for a successor. Many of them are already well known as failures; others are nothing more than bold or avaricious. The new doctor is yet to come. And when he comes, he will use my medicines. He need only use them better. An accuser of Admiral Persano replied, when asked what the admiral was guilty of, Of losing. The same is true of me."

As his power increased, Mussolini became more intolerant of criticism, but his propaganda machine convinced most Italians and foreign statesmen he was the leader to fight off the threat of Communism. There was little Italian protest as freedoms gave way to repressions of a totalitarian state. To Mussolini this was proof the people wanted to be ruled and to be left in peace. The square set jaw, always jutting out in arrogant authority, decried the bellicose nationalism which hid his lack of leadership knowledge and temperament. His health impaired, severe depression compounding his suffering, he began to isolate himself and became a footman to Hitler. He even had his son-in-law executed for voting against him in the Grand Council!"

I continued, "In an interview shortly before his infamous assassination, he proclaimed:"

"I've already told you. The Third World War will break out. Capitalist democracies against Bolshevist capitalism. Only our victory would have brought the world peace with justice. I was accused of tyranny, which I imposed on the Italians. How they will mourn it. And it will have to return, if the Italians want to be a nation again and not a bunch of slaves. And the Italians will want it. They yearn for it. The furious people will chase away the false leaders, the base little men who have submitted to foreign interests. They will carry flowers to the graves of the martyrs, the graves of those who have fallen for an idea, who will be the light and the hope of the world. Then they will say without flattery or falsehood: Mussolini was right!"

"I could not disagree more! In summary, the greatest accomplishment of his public career was to restore Italy's confidence in itself after the devastating experience of World War I. His greatest mistake was to lead Italy into World War II, for which the people, the economy and the military establishment were not adequately prepared. In fact, his entire military command advised him Italy could not possibly be prepared for war until 1949. Il Duce believed insanely he could never be in error. Anyone who agrees with that, raise your hand before I begin my challenge to my fellow students. Let's have a discussion on the intents of these tyrant dictators..."

What was the morality of resistance?

The latter war years and attempts at reconstruction in the "old country" were still very fresh to my family; Tia Tina and the children had left the mother country, Italy, as the breakdown of Mussolini's regime forced Il Duce to resign, saw King Vittorio Emanuele sign an unconditional surrender to the Allies, and then declare war on her former ally, Germany. For the next eighteen months, until liberation day of April 25, 1945 the country would experience the full throes of civil war.

Mussolini had been arrested and imprisoned in mountains at the northern border with Austria. The German occupation reached as far south as Rome and Naples while further to the south were the Allies, beginning their tortuous advance up the mountainous peninsula. So it was, the uncertainty over who actually represented the real Italy created an even deeper division between the "industrial" north and the more agrarian south. Those faithful to the German regime aligned against the partisans who were aligned with the Allies against them. The end of Fascism in Italy, you see, was only the beginning of the turn of tide which led to Allied victory in Europe. The years that followed for Italy have been chaos.

What was the morality of resistance? My home country still had not been purged of its fascist contingent and was flirting with communism. In reflecting on the outcome of war, we are left wondering if the victors were really 'the better', or was the evil Axis no longer up to the fight? Could losses be attributed to blunderous circumstances? Were the battle strategies ill conceived? Or was the win a moral victory evidencing a triumph of good over evil?

With the exception of those self-proclaimed Masters of Destiny, from Mussolini and Hitler back to Cain in Genesis, lives lost in conflicts and warfare would have been lives lived. These would be themes I would mull over for years and would lead me to the profession of photojournalism, enabling me to interview currently significant people in my new home country. I deeply felt I could use my camera and journalistic skills to evoke their responses, from their hearts and histories to awaken in the public their civic responsibility to be vigilant. With a free press we might advance democratic ideals. Censorship only benefits the propagandists. The masses then become the oppressed.

Historiography is the warning that perhaps history begins where memory fails. My photographic career will provide that reminder to all of us, the tragic past can easily become our tragic future.

TWENTY

—◆○◆—

FIVE DARK POINTS OF

FOCUS

Frank caught my attention the moment I arrived at school, the day following my introduction to his parents, wide-eyed, checking to see if I was still joining him to meet his mother this afternoon. I nodded assurance and mouthed, "I can hardly sit through class!" Immediately after the last class bell, we rushed out to the bookstore, where Mrs. Ernst was waiting. She had a cup of tea and offered us a Coca Cola, then set out several photographs of jewelry and gems from her collection, many her original creations.

I began, "Mrs. Ernst, I'm impressed with the exquisitely crafted beauty of these creations and your artistic photographic presentations. I hope you don't mind, but I'm full of questions. Much beyond curiosity, I want to learn about your elaborate and bold jewelry creations, the architectural photos, and camera techniques you used to capture so much detail. Here's my own Leica and photos I've taken since being given this gift. It's nearly identical to your camera, case, lenses and all. My mother's brother, Captain Fabio Militello, showed me what he knew about focus, subject composition, lighting, film and care of the camera. but I've had no one else to help improve my skills. I'm so grateful that you're willing to help me with my number one passion! Photography, history, cooking, baking, and childcare are my loves, in that order."

"I notice from these photos, Julietta, you have a knack for detail and for composition. You must be pretty patient to achieve such excellent settings and provocative subjects, nearly from your earliest shots! We'll begin lessons today, starting with fine tuning skills for an amazing camera. We're so fortunate, and I'm excited to work with you. Frank, any thoughts about this?"

Frank stammered a little and then suggested perhaps, as part of our skill-building meetings, he'd develop a greater interest so he could take architectural photos and sports pictures, especially football, or soccer as it is called in the U.S. "I will learn with your camera, *mutti*, but I'd like one of my own, perhaps an Argus." He took my hand again and added, I'm going to be hanging around with this one for a long time, so sharing her interests could surely add to her interest in me. That's right, isn't it Juli?"

"No disagreement there as usual, since we always spark each other's interests further. I like that about you, Frank. A lot," I ventured.

Mrs. Ernst asked if she and the doctor could have my family join them for dinner at their home, perhaps the following Saturday evening. "Honestly, Julietta, we find you so sweet and smart we'd truly like to get to meet your family and know all of you better. There is much we could share about our beginnings here in Cordoba and our past in Europe. I've written an invitation with time and instructions for finding our home on Calle La Rioja and your mamma can ring me up to confirm. I hope a veal roast with potatoes and red cabbage will appeal to you, but I will comply with requests, as well.

Opening her bag to extract the invitation, she pulled out a folded letter which she said she'd like to share with us. It had been written in May 1946 by her brother Alfred Reicher, living in New York. I wiped alfajore cookie crumbs from my hand to take the invitation and listened as she read to Frank and me.

"In April 1945 the western world has 'discovered' the existence of concentration camps in Nazi Germany. A cry of horror is running through the press of these democratic nations. They could have become aware of all this as early as twelve years ago, from thousands of reports from escaped victims, from books backed up by documentary evidence – the Brown Book, for example. If they hadn't ignored the truth back then, this war with its fifty million dead and devastation throughout Europe might have been prevented."

"Hitler made grandiose promises of a Germany re-born, Divine providence to prevail over the Reich's 1000-year reign, a house, garden and car for every worker. The German people put their faith confidently in the Fuëhrer! Everywhere Aryans experienced a great sense of German-ness, and they allowed this nationalist wave of racism to drown their decency. '*Ein Volk, Ein Reich, Ein Fuëhrer* 'was shouted forth from crowds cheering, joyously! One people, one Reich government, one leader, Hitler!"

"British newspapers reported in 1942 the Germans had killed a million Jews, and credible confirmed reports of Hitler's "final solution" reached Roosevelt's cabinet (which had only one Jew, Henry Morgenthau), but the Assistant Secretary of State saw to it the department stopped relaying such information! In 1944 the liberal New York Daily printed a Soviet journalist's account of the Red Army's discoveries on the Eastern Front, including Auschwitz, where Nazi SS had been executing more than 10,000 people a day. Camps with names "Auschwitz II Birkenau, Dauchau, Bergen-Belsen, Ravensbruck, Mathausen and dozens more where undesirable, detested Jews could be concentrated, thus, "Concentration Camps" -- and then forced to labor in intolerable conditions until they were finally executed, many sent to extermination camps."

"A poll in that same year showed most Americans knew Hitler had killed some Jews, but they could not believe even Nazis would have methodically murdered millions. Journalists, including the highly esteemed Edward R. Murrow, who personally visited Buchenwald, warned them: 'Look around, this is how it starts; the first victims are the good Germans themselves. You will be the next if you don't hurry to help them. Help for European Jewry was slow in coming."

Mrs. Ernst looked up from the letter and mentioned she hoped we were following this news. We affirmed we needed to hear all of it, so she proceeded, "President Roosevelt insisted on Germany's unconditional surrender, not even allowing negotiations ostensibly meant to secure the Jews' release of special military operations to save them. Perhaps it was in the Americans' power to rescue them. They did not lift a hand to do it. Now the world is 'discovering' that Nazis act like Nazis. It won't bring the dead back to life."

"The European experience of liberation is horrendous! It's unimaginable horror everywhere can be seen in millions of people uprooted by the Nazis and Fascists and millions more left homeless as a result of their homes -- entire neighborhoods -- being bombed to toxic rubble. These 'displaced persons' have been trekking across Europe. Liberated?"

Her voice breaking, Mrs. Ernst continued, "Not that the Western world cares, but due to one of the cruelest decisions of the Yalta conference, all refugees were to be returned to their pre-war homelands, forcing two million people to be returned into Russian hands, many to be shot outright as defectors, others to languish for years in the gulags. I have heard every sixth person in Germany alone is a refugee! What would have befallen *us* if we had not scurried out of there? I cry for all the casualties and for what still lies ahead."

Mrs. Ernst quietly re-folded that letter and replaced it in her handbag. In the next moment she put her hand on my shoulder and looked deeply into my eyes, saying, "Julietta, I share this now with you because Frank has made me aware of the frustration and upset you experienced with the whitewashed textbook your class is using. We also witnessed the war in our own hometown, a suburb of Berlin."

"Mrs. Ernst," I began "I have never spoken like this to any Germans whether pro-Hitler or not. To use a word I have only encountered in reading, I am dumbfounded. I don't know where to begin! That letter from your brother is full of audacity and pathos. I know my father also feels deeply unsettled to the point of despair, so full of those deep emotions. But how do you, a German, feel?"

"Julietta and Frank, where do I begin? I find it hard to speak of all we have been through, even to you, my son. I...I... we, must and can and will. Agreed?"

Reaching again into her bag, she brought out a bound booklet entitled <u>Reports on the Nuremberg Trials of the First International Military Tribune for War Crimes committed in World War II.</u> "My brother, Alfred, commented separately about this," as she read from a letter inside the pamphlet. "This digest examines the trial and execution of the Nazi leaders who had not fled Germany after Hitler's death. Law and Justice itself were on trial. Never before had crimes committed by a state been brought before a court, nor had responsibility been established for a nation's acts. Twenty-two high-ranking Nazis were charged with crimes against peace, war crimes, and crimes against humanity, as well as with murder and conspiracy to commit these crimes. Chief Prosecutor, Robert H. Jackson and prosecutors from the Allied nations applied the idea the defendants were representatives of Hitler's regime, conspiring to achieve world domination and engaged in a war of aggression. Is actual justice possible when you have a court that permits a British prosecutor to try a German national before a Soviet judge for crimes committed in Poland? And weren't war crimes committed on all sides?" Her expression puzzled and fraught with concern, Mrs. Ernst let slip, "Oh, it is so complex, all of it! And now the memories flood back, uncontainable."

I assured her we would look forward to the dinner I'd have Mamma confirm, and we'd have more sharing than could be concluded in one evening. My brother, Nico would want a copy of that booklet, so I asked if there were some way I could provide a copy, and she said she'd be sure to have one for us at our dinner. I, of course, was hoping there would be many cordial dinners and get-togethers, for many reasons.

TWENTY-ONE

THE BARRIO AND BEYOND

D r. Ernst picked our family up early Saturday evening and drove us rather rapidly through Boulevards and Avenidas now familiar to us. We had spent barely five minutes with introductions, during which time he removed his hat but kept on his overcoat. Papa grabbed his hat and coat, cueing us to do the same. Mamma grabbed the package of a variety of our favorite home-made cookies, and we settled into the car for a twenty-minute drive that would have taken most drivers at least 5 minutes more -- no exaggeration!

Papa's conversational Spanish was still uncertain, but Mamma just translated and went on conversing, while Nico and I looked out the window of his immaculate car and dreamed of the day when we might also have a car to get around.

The Ernst's house was distinctively different from any home in our barrio, Calle Rioja being an upper-class neighborhood whose architect-designed residences aged quite gracefully. Frank ran out to greet us and take Mamma's package of cookies, which he stuck his nose into, giving out a sigh of obvious approval. He helped me out of the car last and put his hand in mine, *not* as a measure of reassurance. I did not withdraw my hand, nor did I blush. Nico noticed and winked approval I pretended to disregard.

Dr. Ernst introduced his wife, Brenda, to my Papa, Mamma and Nico, then after the rest of the formalities, brandished a beautiful smile for us and said, "*Benvenuto a casa nostra*" in near perfect Italian. It endeared him to my parents immediately. "We have lived in this lovely house for nearly a year, having escaped the vicious grip the Nazis had in Germany and its occupied states. By 'we', I refer to the successful escape of our small family here, Brenda's parents and some of their siblings, and her brother Alfred. Our family paid heavily to enter Belgium and then London. My own parents and their relatives could not flee Germany, but then they are not Jews, like Brenda's family. Herr Hitler had not invented anti-Semitism, but he was a virulent persecutor and executioner intent on full extermination, as you know, I'm sure."

Mrs. Ernst took our jackets to hang up and invited us to tour the home. As we followed her, she said, "We were fortunate the custom jewelry business which my father built and I apprenticed before earning my Master Gemologist certification, provided the generous means for us to make our way here. Raymond has an E.E.N.T. surgical practice downtown, and with the growing immigrant population to Argentina, he has been asked to open a clinic near the University. The University Medical School has contracted with him to mentor interns and residents, which will in time also expand the practice. I have kept a lower profile, as I feel uneasy opening shop in this tense political climate." Almost as an aside, she added, "It's also apparent there are thousands of Germans, nearly everywhere, causing me overwhelming consternation about possible Nazi spies or worse."

"These statements are preliminary to giving you a home tour, since we found this house, expecting it would provide adequate room for family members and friends of ours should they decide to follow us to thriving Cordoba. Here it is 1948 and I still hide documents, jewelry, cash, and letters. There's no excessive paranoia in my certainty that dictators, Fascists, Nazis and Communists are all suspect, and are amongst us in Cordoba, even in this neighborhood!" Mrs. Ernst's last statement elicited concern and then laughter from all of us as Frank followed with, "Great, *Mutti,* but will you please stop looking over your shoulder long enough to give our guests a tour of the house. I'm super hungry for dinner, and it smells so delicious!"

Nico hung back with me and Frank, more interested in the neighborhood than in their specific house. "Frank, you and your mother have mentioned suspicions about the unfriendly Germans and possible Nazi activity right in this neighborhood, so tell us everything you've witnessed and know. I've learned to be suspicious like your *Mutti,* but I have little first-hand evidence of bad intentions, whatever they may be. Does your family fear their numbers might be large enough to create a movement imperiling Argentina's fragile republic?"

"Yes and no. That is, we're generally aware of their gatherings, their 'underground' activities and their continuous providing safe passage for fleeing Nazis, most of them war criminals. But proving it? My father knows for certain the Perón government is regularly assisting these Nazis arriving every week. He hears Perón provides documents and assistance, even cover. For a price, of course."

"And that price is...? Julietta asked.

"I wish I had solid proof of this, but considerable gold, art, jewels, and money stolen from victims of their vicious murderous war crimes has been making its way into this country -- partly through Swiss banks, which have a presence here, and probably right to Casa Rosada, the Presidential Palace whose balcony is the stage for the adored Evita and her thus adored husband, Juan Perón."

Frank went on, "Nico, evil must be clothed, right? I know you have a serious interest in social justice and law, so I ask if you have seen anything cloaked in secrecy but detectably evil?" At this point, the group returned from the upper story and Frank nodded for us to hush, putting his finger to his lips. I felt the oddest urge to put my lips to his, hoping he might be thinking the same thing. I learned soon enough he was!

Mrs. Ernst brought her Leica and some photograph albums down, setting them on the dark chestnut coffee table across from the huge fireplace whose flames softened the lighting in this massive room. She led us to the dining room with another massive chestnut table set with lovely vintage porcelain dinnerware, hand painted raised pink rosettes spreading from painted green leaves. She asked us to take a seat and then spoke of a family with whom they'd been working during their volunteering, having to return permanently to Germany to care for aging parents.

"These plates were heirlooms of theirs, which Dr. Ernst had obligingly agreed to buy at a better than fair price. We all benefitted, though we do miss them, and expect they miss their lovely dinnerware. The family was gone, then, within two days!"

"I wish I could make sense of more odd situations like this, which make me quite uncomfortable, but there isn't a clear explanation for these otherwise unremarkable comings and goings." While Mrs. Ernst went to the kitchen to bring the roast to the table, Dr. Ernst remarked he felt more certain there was an explanation, and said he would like to talk further with us about the Nazi escape route, and about Perónist tactics to keep a cloak over these suspicions. Reportedly, people were even being "disappeared" when they mouthed concern about pro-Nazism evident throughout Argentina, especially at the port of Buenos Aires.

While he was mentioning this, Frank got up to help his mother serve the food and pour the wine, then reached over and gave her a slight kiss and a bright smile. *O, Dio*! I have developed a crush on him.

Following the dessert of linzer torte with its raspberry filling delectably still tingling my tongue, Mrs. Ernst refused help cleaning up and directed us to the fireplace warmed living room, inviting us to make ourselves at home, saying, "We have, it seems, more in common than just the friendship between Frank and Julietta. Really, Raymond and I have loved getting to know Julietta and her passion for truth and learning. What put my interest over the top was she and I share love of photography with our nearly identical Leica cameras. The afternoon we spent at the bookstore earlier this week went so fast, my teaching her the next level of camera technique, and she showing me photos she had taken, from the earliest of her circle in Vietri sul Mare through the latter pictures taken here in Cordoba. What a talent she has for composition, detail and subject!"

Papa proudly added his daughter tells stories through photography, "Julietta has a future in photojournalism, with power to put the audience in someone else's shoes. I see her bridging differences in social stratification, consequently spurring social change. Angelina and I felt certain of this when buying the Leica through the discreet network of 'black market' goods accessible to higher echelon career military officers, specifically Angelina's brother, Captain

Fabio. We surmised and hoped it would provide her the wings to soar into the vast world of words and images."

"I would add she is a model in taking inspiration from diverse sources, like Life magazine, documentaries and texts, culture, especially history. Whew! She is already a powerhouse and is barely starting high school studies. Raymond and I have a collection of periodicals to share with you, sitting next to your chair, Carmine. You can return them when you have read them, sharing some of your own with us." Mrs. Ernst then picked through a few, commenting on them:

Time, U.S. edition 21/6/43 Mussolini cover photo, wearing a halo of Italy

Time (*Tempo*) 24/6/40 Mussolini with Badoglio

Life 24/7/44 Life and Times looking back on the destruction of Italian cultural heritage in WWI; more Life:

12/6/44 Landing in Italy

3/2/41 War News from Inside Germany

13/5/40 Il Duce: Key Man of the Mediterranean

"We have many more so don't be reserved about asking. Julietta has already pored over these, leading to technical questions about the photographs I don't have the understanding, myself, to answer. But she got me so curious I asked my brother Alfred to lead us in some learning sessions. While in New York, he has earned a doctorate in Journalism and is on the faculty of New York University. If there was a degree in integrity and exposing lies, Alfred would have earned that as well."

"Brenda, are you saying he will be here in Cordoba? Julietta and Frank have spoken about his courage and astuteness from letters he's sent you. When do you expect him, and when is the last time you have seen him?" asked my Mamma. She was intrigued, making me wonder if she was thinking of Fabio and deeply missing him. I guess I might even feel that way should Nico and I be separated by oceans, but I wasn't so certain.

"He will be here at the end of fall term in May, staying for three weeks, and yes, I miss him terribly, not having seen him for three years already. He introduced Raymond and I, and was best man at our wedding. He's also my sole surviving brother and I fear for him. N.Y.U. is a liberal college, so he feels he can espouse views of the kind that will surely get him in trouble here."

"My brother, Paolo can set him straight on what he had better not let escape from his lips, just as he tried to do with Nico and me when we first arrived!" Papa spoke this and caused us all to laugh, then added, "Dissidents, both the outspoken and many unknowns have been disappearing from Argentina and there's no trace of them. This is happening under Perón's direction, and the military are known to be at the root of these kidnappings. Nico's closest friends are careful not to be overheard, but they are revolutionary intellectuals at the university. Anything potentially subversive could make one a suspect. Who can even tell when someone might be listening, or worse?"

Nico spoke on behalf of his revolutionary *compadres*, "We are not malcontents, but as we become more aware of the tightening noose of authoritarianism held by Perón and his cadres and thugs, we have formed a group to remain vigilant, share information and rumors, and devise plans to reveal these threats to life and liberty. Yes, it is that bad!"

Frank felt the subject was becoming more ominous than genial, so asked if we might like a short walk for fresh air. Nico and I accepted, knowing he also wanted to steer us away from discussions of such magnitude that we might end the evening in a serious state of discomfort. Good move, as when we returned, the parents were smiling and writing down a date for the Ernst's to have dinner at our home in Barrio Guemes, next week!

Mrs. Ernst motioned us all back into the living room to show some of the fine gold and gem creations she had brought from Germany. I had seen some of these in her photographic collection, but I was totally dazzled to see them in person. As my parents were bent admiringly over the collection, I went to see what Frank was up to, nearer to the kitchen. Surprise overtook me as he grabbed my arm and snatched me into the library/study while everyone else was deeply engaged in the living room.

I loved being pulled entirely close to him so I wrapped both arms around his neck bringing our bodies close and our faces closer. I barely had time to engage his eyes with mine when, as I closed my eyes, his mouth grasped mine, and eagerly parted my lips. Several moments of this, and I let my tongue slip between his parted lips.

Hearing the group moving about from the living room, we moved aside and in my ear he said, "Yum! An Italian girl eagerly responding to her German boyfriend with a French kiss! How European, and in Argentina!"

Nobody noticed when my boyfriend and I returned, as they hadn't been aware we'd gone missing. I hoped they wouldn't notice my pounding heart!

TWENTY-TWO

HIGH CULTURE IN BUENOS AIRES

D r. and Mrs. Ernst had just returned to Cordoba with Brenda's brother Alfred, whom they drove from his flight into Buenos Aires a few days before. While in Buenos Aires, they stealthily scoped out neighborhoods where suspected Nazi fugitives, smuggled in through "rat lines" would have been kept hidden until they could be given false identities and become part of the wealthy and powerful political mafia. Many others were sent on to Neuquén, Patagonia, La Plata, or Cordoba. Mrs. Ernst took pictures of suspected homes, while photographing cafés, monuments, government buildings, palaces, parks and shops, as if she were an innocent tourist. She most certainly was anything but that! When those photos were developed, she would use them as further evidence of the web of Nazi infiltration into post-war Argentina.

The trio attended a world class performance of Verdi's Aida in full Egyptian regalia, at the stunningly ornate Opera House, Teatro Colón, then treated themselves to watching a Tango competition at the Marriott Hotel in Buenos Aires, where it was first performed. The music was loud, vivid, and certainly sexual in its overtures and its appeal to the audience, dancers and performers. They recognized several Tango pieces made famous by Carlos Gardel, who popularized the lyrics and music into a world-acclaimed art form.

Alfred left his wine glass on the table but stubbed out his half-smoked cigarette as he explained he'd be back as soon as he could complete his "inspired piece" on the typewriter the Marriott supplied for him to use in their sixth floor suite. This is the piece he submitted and had published with photos his sister had taken, in the Saturday Evening Post three weeks later:

The Tango

Witness the seductively attractive dancers in unison, coupling, with ankle taps, foot sweeps, swoons, and waist cinches! Partners entice each other and NEVER lose engagement. Oh, she may turn her back and he may look aside, but it is in furtherance of their finely coordinated moves. The tango has not a wasted movement or gesture; each partner beckons the other and the audience from the moment the dance commences.

His hand is positioned flat against her back just behind her heart. Passion pours out into the audience and intensifies the musicians! Tonight's quartet, which includes two deft violinists, a singer/temptress and a bandoneon player, said to be the best in Argentina, needed no percussion. The instruments woo you as the dancers take the spotlight, traversing the entire dance floor, moving to their partner's breath and swelling sounds of the strings.

Her dress, black taffeta with three successive flounces where her hips and thighs seemed poured into, cascades down to the knee. And those large, spiraled ruffles beg to be swirled to expose flesh, the cause for observers to want to lay down at her feet and smother those vividly taut legs with kisses. Her daring red dance shoes perform their own seduction, enhanced by the severe cut of her black bangs and long hair that swings perfectly with her angular bare shoulders. The ivory silk bodice is scalloped, framing her breasts and exposing their pure fine shape nearly to the nipples, causing the audience to gasp each time her head to her waist bent gracefully back like a swan in a mating pose.

His dance outfit, black pants fitted loosely to tall athletic legs is cummerbund-wrapped in red satin, perfectly matching her shoes, lipstick and crystal laden hair ornament. Matching as well is his ivory satin shirt adorned with large jet-black buttons that shoot light back at the beauty he holds, even as his eyes shoot fiery glances directly into hers. Their individual worlds are suspended in ice, as the dance heats the participants, that is everyone in the room.

Alfred arranged with the front desk clerk, while flashing her his most sincere smile and cash, to have the piece air-mailed to the editor of the Post. Then he rejoined the Ernst's at their table on the edge of the dance floor and quickly became mesmerized by the many couples sweeping past them. After enjoying a few more cocktails, Brenda pulled Alfred onto the dance floor as the lead singer promised to teach tango lessons to anyone brave enough to join in. Clumsiness and an unintended wicked kick had them both exploding in laughter but also had Dr. Ernst applauding as they developed a tributable couples' dance which they promised to repeat on subsequent visits, sealed with the toasts, "*Prost*" and "*Zum Wohl*" for proverbial good health.

Steeped in the colonial ambience of the Marriott where they had spent two nights, they had much to talk about while driving to Cordoba, a ten-hour trip. They remained suspended between exposing covert dangers and reliving the visions of their Buenos Aires adventures, filling chasms of their years of separation, and setting a course for their future.

Once their honored and much-loved guest settled in, the Ernst's asked us to stop by for coffee (Alfred did not like maté) and dessert at their house, with Dr. Ernst chauffeuring us round trip. During that drive, Raymond disclosed information we had not known, including Alfred had served on the prestigious Committee Investigating Un-American Activities, specifically the "Red Threat", and he'd brought his parents to the United States where they settled in his apartment in New York while he was studying. Fortuitously they found a cottage near the lower Hudson River, just outside the boroughs, that provided for them a calmer late in life environment, and was also a retreat for Alfred. Their prayers to be reunited with Brenda, Raymond and Frank were yet to be realized, but Dr. Ernst intimated they shared their hope to make this happen within a year.

"I hesitate to share with you details of the life we fled under Hitler's Nazi state, as you have under Mussolini's catastrophic war. But since sensitive subjects might be spoken of during Alfred's visit, and most certainly will be over the upcoming months as we come to know each other better, I will mention some now. As you know, Mrs. Ernst is a Jew, whose family led a prosperous life from their jewelry business and were highly regarded in academic and intellectual circles. They were not socialites, and certainly not troublemakers. From the years that I was in secondary school, Brenda's brother David had been my closest friend. He was as much a trickster as he was a quick-witted intellectual, and more loyal a friend than anyone I have known since. David was my confidante when I married his sister Brenda and he always chided me I ought to have had a sister as amazing as her so he could marry his ideal mate. The night of Krystallnacht, he and I from the shadows watched in horror and fear as the S.S. broke shopfront windows of **all** Jewish merchants, provoking growing, angry crowds to join the riot. I rushed to David's house to fetch his father and brother to salvage whatever we could. Fortunately, Brenda's father always set the valuable jewelry into the large safe in the back office, as what followed was an unthinkable melee. The very neighbors and customers who considered the Reicher's their trusted jewelers, looted and damaged the premises. The SS then wrote *Juden*, the German for Jew, and swastikas all over the shops."

Mr. Ernst was too choked up to continue and none of us would have pushed him to re-live those events he would surely have preferred to forget. But as we neared his house, he slowed down and told us more, "It was David who insisted we leave our homeland without delay, and found passage for Brenda, Frank and me to Argentina. Alfred arranged passage for himself and his parents to New York. David insisted on staying behind and selling anything left in our homes before joining us. He never achieved that...the Nazis rounded up Jews beginning with that event and shipped the best friend I've ever had to Dachau, and I fear on to Malthausen, a death camp. We owe everything to him!" My Papa drew his handkerchief from his inner coat pocket and handed it to Raymond, who by then had pulled into his parking space at his home. Mamma and I felt tears softly rolling down our faces.

TWENTY-THREE

SPOTLIGHT ON BROADCAST

JOURNALISM

A lfred Reicher was a middle-aged gentleman, short and unremarkable in appearance. He had none of the "airs" of a distinguished scholar and professor despite carrying a briefcase. He laughed when I mentioned, upon first meeting him, "Lacking the appearance and accoutrements of your profession, you look quite ordinary, keeping you above suspicion, right?"

"I keep a notebook in an inside pocket sewn into my jacket, because I like to record times, places and statements that arouse my suspicions. These notes will serve as the basis for later research and articles I intend to publish in journals read mostly by academics."

I blurted out, "I am a student of journalism and photography, and I'm working on my first submission to the newsletter of my brother, Nico's university. His girlfriend, Luca is the primary author, and our topic is the spread of Social Democratic ideals amongst college students. It's totally intriguing when, in interviews with students and faculty, both we and people we interview become more curious about the topic and each other, and recognize the moral evolution that can occur when we really hear each other."

Professor Reicher nodded in knowing agreement.

"Okay, Julietta, how about we all have an opportunity to be properly introduced and engage Mr. Reicher in conversation." My Papa said with a wink and a scratching of his cheek, which I recognized meant I should stop dominating the occasion. It's an Italian thing, I think, so I wasn't embarrassed, but I took the cue and bided my time.

I rarely saw Papa take such an interest in avidly conversing with anyone, yet no one could get a word in as the two of them, joined by Raymond, spoke of life and politics in the United States. Dr. Reicher rifled through papers he'd placed within reach earlier for talking points this evening. "America, the world is watching and trusting you to lead the thrust asking all citizens to despise tyranny in all its forms!" How's that for a call to arms! This is the paper I've submitted to the New York Times, The Los Angeles Times and all the papers that are heavy hitters as well as regional and independents through the Associated Press. It is being featured at the national convention of the Society of Professional Journalists hosted by New York University in two months. I will be presenting along with Edward R. Murrow, whose eminence as a war correspondent and broadcast journalist is unsurpassed. His name is synonymous with courage and perseverance in the search for truth, and he's been credited with changing history. It was his speech in 1929 that urged college students to become more involved in national and world affairs, and influenced me to enter the career of journalism. The upcoming symposium I mentioned will bring together other notables -- giants, actually -- as Charles Collingwood, Howard K. Smith, and William Shirer. They have brought about a revolution in broadcast journalism with World News Roundup, shown on networks around the world on Sunday evenings."

"Wouldn't miss it," chimed in my Papa, who then added, "My family listened to all of Murrow's programs, most notably his live broadcast on 15 April 1945, from the U.S. troops' liberation of the Buchenwald extermination camp in Germany. As you know, this camp provided slave labor for the Reich's armaments industry, and murdered over 56,000 rounded up from Jewish ghettoes and mansions, political enemies, and many others identified by the Reich as undesirables, all less than humans!"

My papa got quite worked up as he continued, "Just days before, the prisoners stormed the watchtowers, seizing control of the camp. U.S. forces then entered, filming and documenting Nazi crimes against humanity. Murrow's report described the emaciated physical state of prisoners who had survived, also describing rows of bodies stacked up like cordwood. In a severely harsh tone, Murrow said he prayed we would believe what he saw and heard, and added if anyone listening was offended, he was not in the least bit sorry."

Professor Reicher nodded his head and said, "To add to that, as American forces closed in on that Nazi concentration camp, Gestapo headquarters at nearby Weimar telephoned the camp administration to announce it was sending explosives to blow up any evidence of the camp -- including its inmates. What the Gestapo did not know was camp administrators had already fled in fear of the Allies. Ya! A prisoner answered the phone and informed headquarters explosives would not be needed, as the camp had already been blown up, which was not true!"

Mrs. Ernst looked with great respect at her brother and spoke up about Edward R. Murrow, "He's a heavy hitter and a heavy smoker, like all others of prominence in this industry. That's why photojournalism is dominated by women. They tend not to stand smoke-filled newsrooms and often are out in the field taking daring photographs. A noble profession, but I personally presume most of those women smoke as well. Carmine and Angelina, you will have to steer Julietta away from that part of the photojournalist' club and their bad habits!"

Mamma looked at me as she chuckled, and concluded this discussion with, "I have a favorite quote from Mr. Murrow. 'A nation of sheep will beget a government of wolves.' That's certainly relevant in every epoch of history and every republic, right up to here and now!"

Professor Reicher added his favorite Murrow quote, "If none of us ever read a book that was 'dangerous,' had a friend who was 'different,' or joined an organization that advocated 'change,' we would all be the kind of people Joe McCarthy wants." Nico piped in, "And the kind of people who have least to fear under Perón!"

Dinner was served, stories were shared, and ideals were placed on a silver platter, for this was a night of vulnerability, wherein we entered into deeper friendships, Alfred being the catalyst. When he asked, before we departed if we had the courage to commit to living from our principles and values, in the face of advancing tyranny, it was like Elijah calling down fire from the heavens. There was no doubt we would stand in agreement, and assuredly would not fall for lies and false beliefs which others ate up. Promises of benefits that would never materialize and messages of false bravado would not deter us from higher goals. Not after a rousing night like this!

The night before Professor Reicher returned to New York was one I could never forget, as Frank placed a pretty blue topaz ring on my hand, and we became steadies. Mrs. Ernst had set the stone, Royal Blue in a simple gold band with a gold surround holding it. She and Frank knew my taste for bold simplicity, and I couldn't stop stealing looks at it on my hand. At Easter, Nico and Luca had become steadies, with him placing on her finger a fire opal from Australia, bought from Brenda Ernst's purloined collection, custom set in a gold band with six raised gold prongs setting it high enough for light to show its sparkles whichever way she moved her hand.

I couldn't wait to show off my ring and my beau to Tio Paolo's entire family that night, walking to their house after my parents gave us their wholehearted blessings. Frank had confided to them he'd be visiting that night, intending to surprise me, and they never let their guard drop, so I was the only one in shock! I rang up my cousin Christiana to be sure her family would be expecting us, as I would ostensibly be bringing them fresh flowers from Mamma's autumn garden. My cousins Christiana and Ana were untypically clandestine about my surprise, so the "oohs and aahs" were genuine, and the warm acceptance of Frank was characteristic of an Italian family. I was grateful Tia Tina gave Tio Paolo that "you'd better not make any embarrassing comments or questions" glance. Christiana told me, in confidence, her papa, last week had asked Silvia's date, a German fellow, if he was going to speak to the family in Spanish or Italian, as he would not have any German spoken in his household!

At the door, Frank made a bowing gesture to Tio Paolo, replying "Mucho gusto," to Paolo's "Buenos tardes." They seemed to be off to a good start.

TWENTY-FOUR

A MORAL EVOLUTION

Tio Paolo's fiftieth birthday fell on the most beautiful early fall day, May 8, 1948. It was also the third anniversary of a day the world could never forget, V.E. Day. Victory in Europe became real with the unconditional surrender of Germany. What occurred that evening was a most potent discussion between the two Migliore families. Tio Paolo had read the manual Nico gifted him last week for his birthday, a book about the "Founding Fathers" of the United States featuring the Declaration of Independence and the Constitution of the United States of America with its Bill of Rights. There seemed a different demeanor in my uncle as he guided everyone to be seated in the living room.

While Paolo assumed his customary role of patriarch, I had never seen him so humble as when he directed Nico to sit next to him and asked the rest of us to gather around. Holding the book with both hands, Paolo remarked that reading this gift changed more in his judgment and way of thinking than words and discussions alone ever had. "Maybe I don't agree with everything the U.S. Constitution declares, like ...all men are created equal. The Italians are maybe more than equal, in my eyes, but if the point is equal justice under the law, that I agree with."

"If I'd read these documents before having my position supporting our President Perón challenged for the past several weeks by Matteo, I would've remained stuck in my beliefs. My little brother, Carmine, loaned some of his Life magazines to my Political Scientist son, Matteo, prompting his commitment to show me the basis for my short-sighted following of presidente Juan Perón. Jesus Christ, I have had *un testa in giù*, and I should be dizzy, having had my world view turned *topsy-turvy*!"

"So, I know I have proclaimed the same sentiments of all the Cordebese union members and community, this regime has fostered the beneficial source of unification of Argentinean politics, with inclusiveness of its immigrants. Was I wrong in believing the Peróns would 100% uphold principles of equal rights for all people? I've witnessed uplifting of the middle class, and greater opportunities respecting laborers, and I don't feel these agendas are insincere gestures. What Matteo has shown me is the darker side of Perón which becomes more oppressive every month, more threatening to our freedoms and rights. Previously, I would have defended our president, but since the arrest of the three young union members at the meat plant on trumped up charges, it became sickeningly clear their arrest was another political maneuver to silence dissidence." Tio Paolo had everyone's attention. He asked Matteo to help him out by outlining facts which led to the conclusion Perón's shadow activities are signs of a possible impending crowning of dictatorship.

Matteo, nodding as his papa was speaking, began, "I needed only to recall and outline increasingly reprehensible activities of the regime, pointing to near certainty Perón's stronghold on all matters of politics and governance was approaching tyranny, more than his façade of benevolence implied. My papa has always been a staunch advocate for democratic values of truth, justice and freedom, so witnessing erosion of those fundamental rights, under Perón's increasing authoritarianism, has been difficult for him, as for most Argentineans. It's just inconsistent with the image of Juan and Evita as exemplary leaders of our Republic."

Matteo picked up a magazine and continued, "This Life article in the 26 June 1944 issue under 'People Make News in the Midst of War', proclaimed Colonel Juan Domingo Perón 'The Boss of Argentina' with a likeness dead-on to Il Duce! Here, I'll read a portion and pass it around. 'Never without manicure, shave and shine, War Lord Peron has the winning manners of a movie football hero and the mind of an intelligent gambler. On the day Rome fell there opened in Buenos Aires, Perón's exact imitation of a Mussolini rally...and over all, Perón's own symbol for Argentina: a huge figure of a condor with wings outspread like the Nazi eagle.' My papa studied that as he grumbled to me about how the likeness is more than skin deep. Like Mussolini, Perón's intention is covertly to win over the middle class and poor so he can become a dictator as well! Papa and I have had some deep conversations about Populism and its next stage, Authoritarianism, right up to tonight!"

Tia Tina, studying her husband's face, spoke up, "I think we've been letting the social progress and labor victories of improved wages, hours, and benefits, and having a voice, blind us to political maneuverings surely meant to control us! President Perón has been exploiting the working class for the sake of his own ambitions! His success results from their unequivocal support for his reforms and their wrongly placed devotion to him."

"*Mamacita*," said Christiana, "Well spoken! Argentineans are new to democratic principles, but as Italians, our recent history of being easily distracted by progress, 'bread and circuses,' and applauding the leader as our savior, well, these should serve as evidence of a despotic leader's pretense at democracy. Last year when Perón proclaimed the rights and dignity of the *descamisados* in the Bill of Rights of the Workers of Argentina, he also created a large propaganda apparatus; his regime offers free university education to all who qualify, while he purges more than half the professors, and forbids political activity on campus. Workers are happily in agreement that *'Perón cumple'*, 'Perón delivers', but all my friends and I see President Perón's reforms are veiled policies to further his control over all Argentina. Look at how, until now, the workers have enthusiastically exclaimed his popularity while their wages increased and he has uplifted them into the middle class. Perónist masses of 'New Argentina', have avoided mention of his silencing journalists and legitimate news sources, censoring the media, and, we all suspect, rigging elections to increase his own powers. He has re-written student textbooks -- how low can he go? What crap we have been fed!"

My Tio Paolo then revealed a transformation, something I had never witnessed in any circumstances except educational settings or in grieving a dear one's sudden loss. To his credit, there was neither challenging nor boasting, but a new wisdom shone through. Looking from his daughter to Nico, Tio Paolo cleared his throat and said, "I ask your forgiveness, Salvatore. I've shortchanged you consistently and never gave your ideas much credence. My family has heard me spout off, sometimes interminably, about politics – the systems, institutions and people I know something about. While not having considerable education, I never saw myself as ignorant. I have been! I want to be a better man and I want to live in a better Argentina. My world view has changed!" The silence which followed was quizzically solemn.

Minutes later Paolo spoke to all of us: "I love the community I've helped build right here in Barrio Guemes, Cordoba's Roma... and I love the opportunities Argentina's industries and institutions have made available to me and my family and millions of immigrants. We have respect! We have liberties. We are important to this country. When our two families compare our home back in Vietri sul Mare with our home here in Cordoba, I have stuck out my chest boasting how I've made a wonderful life for us in two countries."

Tia Tina nearly dropped the tray of antipasto she was carrying towards us during Paolo's admissions. She took an audibly deep breath, composed herself and said, "Don't pay attention to me. I'm as astounded as the rest of you! Pass the tray. It may be a while before dinner is served!"

Tio Paolo snorted lightly but returned to his confession, "Having now read the preamble to the Constitution of the United States, and the Declaration of Independence, I recognize more clearly the shortcomings of our adopted country - truthfully its vices – are never fully reported, or even spoken of amongst our people. We should be calling them out as the evils under authoritarianism. Democracy has hit many craters, mostly at the hands of rogue presidents who centralize power and trample the law. Hell, here in Argentina, they put in place lawmakers who change the constitution, furthering the aims of their latest dictator. I have denied the truth for too long, and I agree with you and Carmine we must call out tyranny for what it is and listen to what America to the north has created to avoid the inherent evils of despotism."

Sitting around their fireplace once we had sung 'Happy Birthday' and cake plates were cleared away, my uncle handed the book back to Nico, while everyone waited, tentative and curious. Tio Paolo lowered his tone when he asked, "Salvatore, please read from The Declaration of Independence, signed by America's great statesmen in 1776."

Nico knew the words by heart and spoke them, book on his lap. "We hold these truths to be self-evident. That all men are created equal. That they are endowed by their creator with certain inalienable rights. That among these are life, liberty and the pursuit of happiness. That to secure these rights, governments are instituted among men deriving their just powers from the consent of the governed. That whenever any form of government becomes destructive of these ends, it is the right of the people to alter or to abolish it and to institute a new government, laying its foundations on such principles and organizing its powers in such form as to them shall seem most likely to effect their safety and happiness. Prudence, indeed, shall determine that governments long established, shall not be changed for light and transient causes; and accordingly, all experience has shown that mankind is more disposed to suffer while evils are sufferable than to right themselves by abolishing the forms to which they are accustomed. But when a long train of abuses and usurpations, pursuing invariably the same object, evinces a design to reduce them under absolute despotism, it is their right, it is their duty, to throw off such government and to provide new guards for their future security."

"Hamilton's ongoing fear was that American democracy would be spoiled by demagogues who would mouth populist sayings to conceal their despotism" Nico added.

Hardly waiting for Nico to finish, Papa took up the reasoned arguments by adding, "Remember that German propaganda film. "Triumph of the Will"? It was shot by the film-star, who become Hitler's favorite filmmaker. Leni -- I can't remember her last name -- in 1935."

I broke in, "Papa, that was Helene Riefenstahl! She used gorgeous images of Germany, raising high Wagner's motifs of power and beauty. Famously, she was given unlimited resources and full artistic license to make this masterful propaganda film. She won Best Foreign Film award at the Venice Film Festival!"

Papa winked at me, smiling, then smirking as he continued, "*Danke, mein fraulein*! I've followed her because I still cannot believe so accomplished a professional could be lured into *'der Fuhrer's Reich'* of lies and evil. In an interview she said, to her, 'Hitler was the greatest man who ever lived, without fault, and possessed of masculine strength.' Reportedly she had been riveted by his oratorical style and his ability to mesmerize audiences. Well, she became a war correspondent in Poland in 1939. Witnessing execution of thousands of Polish civilians shot in retaliation for a partisan attack on German troops, Fraulein Riefenstahl made a personal appeal to her Fuehrer against this unnecessary violence, but it did not prevent her from filming Hitler's triumphal parade into Warsaw just weeks later."

"Carmine, that is very interesting, but I'm curious. What are you suggesting?" asked Mamma. "She bought into, and polished the Nazi propaganda, yes, but none of us here are so 'mesmerized' by Perón."

Papa told the rest of the story, revealing its relevance. "The French authorities occupying the Tyrol, arrested Fraulein Leni and confiscated her film materials in 1946. She was declared a Nazi sympathizer whose visions were essential to carrying out the mission for elimination of millions of Jews and 'other undesirables' during the regime. Do you know she later 'recanted' to placate those who would implicate her in war crimes, by saying she was one of millions who thought Hitler had all the answers? Millions of Germans who saw only the good things and 'didn't know' bad things were to come. How many amongst the Cordobese and the rest of Argentina similarly revere their leader, and are riveted by his and his wife's style, mesmerized to the extent they will not see how bad things are now and worse to come?"

Paolo muttered, "We've just been discussing the foundations for a democratic republic, and now we need to add the threat of unwittingly supporting a despot. I hadn't even made up my mind that Perón is a despot!"

Matteo and Nico exchanged glances and simultaneously whistled "Yankee Doodle," starting everyone laughing like crazy. Matteo made the next comments, "Dictatorship granted too easily with populist support usually becomes despotism. Germany, Italy, Russia, and Argentina are among the most recent examples of where this leads to -- the demagoguery of despots was foremost in the minds of the American colonists who came together as Patriots. They took action, underscored by the words of the Declaration of Independence, 'evincing a design to reduce the abuses and usurpations under absolute despotism,' and founded a constitutional republic amidst the most unsettling of times."

Raising a fist in the air, Nico retorted emphatically, "A revolutionary war ensued. It had to! *Viva la democracia*! Those of us who have been choked with the shame and rubbish of war declared by despots with the deceived populist support of their respective citizens need to look to this document and hold democracy dear." Nico's words left everyone smiling as they nodded in comprehension and agreement.

Papa pulled himself up, waved for us to get a move on, and we gave everyone air kisses and hugs for the night. "What a way to celebrate your birthday and next half century of new thinking for you, *i mei fratello*! May you live that long!"

Offhandedly and with the humor found between Italian family members, Tio Paolo said to his younger brother, "*Si sono piene di merda, ma ti amo!*" and Papa replied as he walked us out the door, "You are even more full of shit, but I love you, even for that!"

We had stayed so long after dropping Mamma and Papa back home, Matteo came back with their car to drive Frank home. As we walked back to our home, Nico began conversing with me more as his peer than as his little sister. I sensed respect, I knew much had changed, and without acknowledging it, we left our childhood ways behind us.

TWENTY-FIVE

SECRET TRUTHS

I noticed since I turned 16, I have become more apprehensive about speaking to anyone not in our most trusted circle in Cordoba. When Mamma mentioned she would like to invite the Weiss family over to our home for dinner, I suggested instead we take a picnic lunch to an outdoor concert in the park this weekend. "The kids and I can rollick about while the adults can talk serious matters. Nico spends most weekends with Luca and his friends, and I'd find it awkward to sit around a dining table once again, especially now their kids are older and love to play tag and throw a ball. Running outdoors will be better than being cooped up at an evening dinner."

Mamma thought for a few minutes and said she got my point. "Marta has been hinting, if not outright asking, to visit me at our home, so first I may invite just her and Albert over for a Sunday evening Italian meal. Did I tell you they have found a sweet rental cottage just inside the beltway, close to Albert's job at the University Institute of Aeronautics. Il *Instituto Universitario Aeronautico* has already been recognized as a very distinguished agency of the Argentine Air Force in its second year as an educational center. He must be very talented to have been selected as an engineer on their faculty!"

"Mamma, I don't see your friendship with Marta as a good fit. She's brash and not forthcoming in a genuine way, as you are. In the year since we left them at the Buenos Aires dock, Marta has finagled her way into our lives, in an opportunistic way. I thought little of it when they were staying at the residence hotel last year, after their move to Cordoba, but it seems odd she continues to prefer your company to making friends of her own age, friends with children of similar ages to hers. No offense, Mamma, but often I feel she has "*nella manica*," you know, something up her sleeve. When I used to go by and take care of the children for her, she would hang around when I wanted to leave, and ask me questions. I tell you nearly everything, but thinking about some of her odd conversations, maybe now is the time to get your feedback."

"Shoot, Juli! I'd rather piece together your suspicions with my own observations and see where this is leading. You know I'm not thin-skinned, so no offense on my part." Mamma handed me the dishtowel to wipe dishes she was washing. "We need to finish up lunch dishes pronto so we can make a tray of capocollo and roast beef sandwiches and slice the provolone for tonight's meeting at Luca's bookstore. I have the marinated eggplant and cherry peppers ready and had the bread pre-sliced to save time."

I called out to her, "I'll finish up clearing dishes and making the sandwich platter, Mamma. Maybe that will give you time to complete your assignment and read at least a portion of it to me. You are such an inspiration! I mean for the lifetime of recognition I have seen you always stand strong, wise, and compassionate and I recognize your thoroughness and skills as you take on sometimes extraordinary projects. Raising Nico must be one of those, Mamma. Just kidding!"

After flicking my butt with a dishtowel, she replaced her apron on the hook beside the range. Walking to her chair, it wasn't clear whether Mamma was still speaking to me or to herself. "I need to finish my 'Nazis in Argentina' assignment." She was referring to the researched written reports each participant in Luca's bookstore revolutionary group would be reading -- reports which would elucidate the why's and where's of the alarming, growing presence of Nazis in Argentina.

I knew she was speaking to me when, over her shoulder she clearly said, "Papa could hardly restrain himself from completing his assigned report he calls Devastation to Hope on the miserable, desolate days the 8 May 1945 Peace Agreement left the suffering Italians. Conditions which have polarized the provocateurs -- as defeated Axis countries are now being called -- to seek relief from punishments and impossibility of rebuilding lives. Italian citizens of our new republic had dismal choices: Social Democrats, Christian Democrats, or Communists? Remain in our *patria*, or depart to offer our children more promising futures? Accept hefty remunerations demanded by the Allies for the devastation caused by Hitler and Mussolini, or try to re-negotiate less punitive terms?"

Mamma resumed her project, placed on the side table in the living room, facing the altar with its Infant of Prague. She crossed herself before starting, and I watched her intensity composing brilliant, though, without hard evidence, inconclusive insights. Once all the reports were compiled, conclusions drawn would be terrifying, and explicate cause for disdain towards our Church, but not diminish our love for Our Lord.

Before she finished, she asked me to sit down and listen to what she had written up to that point, "We may not be the most fashionable amongst the Italian immigrants, those more middle class calling themselves Italo-Argentineans, but more importantly, our family -- each of us -- is educated. As continuous learners, we seek out unbiased literary sources, like we find in Papa's Life and Look magazines, Chronache di Guerra and Tempo from back home. I value our small collection of books, some of which have been banned, usually burned, in Germany, Poland, Italy, even here! Books themselves considered anti-Fascist, or their authors considered subversive. These make us more informed and conversant about non-propagandized current events."

I broke in, "Great start, Mamma! I'm intrigued to hear the rest."

"So, with factual and intensely serious findings supplied by the Ernst's and more information I have collected, I am consolidating all I could find to support the undeniable truth of a large and very sinister Nazi presence in Argentina. It all points to the Nazi elites, the SS especially, having been given safe passage here with support of the Perón government, Swiss banks and businessmen, the Italian and Spanish governments, and most ashamedly, the Vatican and Roman Catholic Church. Imagine men of God using their faith as weapons, tools to further an agenda which rewards evildoing! I believe that makes them co-conspirators of the murderous violence carried out under Hitler's orders. *It shakes me to the core!*"

Papa and Nico arrived home minutes after Mamma finished her report, sporting suspicious grins. What secret they were hiding from us, they were determined to keep sealed between them, so while we waited for Matteo to pick us up for the evening meeting at R.E.L.L., Mamma told them about our earlier discussion and her decision to have Albert and Marta over on a Sunday evening. Hearing Matteo's knock at the door, I noticed that Papa jabbed Nico in the side and they both tried to contain that same silly secret. "*Ciao!* How goes it -- is everybody ready?" was Matteo's regular greeting, except for a glance to the men and wink he shot in their direction.

We grabbed our reports and trays of food and headed for the car. Except it wasn't Tio Paolo's six-year-old sedan, but a newer black Ford waiting for us, and Matteo handed the keys to Papa!

"*O mio Dio*! It can't be!" Mamma declared, realizing right away this had to be *our* car. While everyone laughed, she piped in, "I can't wait to learn to drive!" She embraced and kissed Papa right there at the curb and he made the sign "ok" with his fingers to Matteo and Nico. I always had my camera with me, so I snapped a few photos, finishing the roll so I could have the film processed and mail prints to my Nonni -- I wished so hard they could have been here for this happy occasion!

We pulled into the service alley behind Luca's Bookstore and Nico ran around to the front so he could enter through the ornately carved archway. Moments later, he brought Luca out the back door. She jumped up and down as she noticed Papa driving the new car, and the realization he had bought it. Walter concluded a book sale and dashed out back to witness all of this, smiling to be part of an occasion which wasn't ominous, like some from our past and more we expected to come.

The mood switched from exhilaration to dismay when Mamma commenced a conversation with Brenda. Mrs.

Ernst had been feeding my family whatever information she received from her brother, and from German immigrants she worked with in the Mutual Aid Benevolence Society. Most notable was secret information conveyed to her by Dr. Ernst, who, while appearing to be totally absorbed in his own business, was vigilantly memorizing conversations overheard at adjoining tables in cafés he frequented. His professional appearance belied the threat he really posed to German speaking regulars, clearly still pro-Nazi, and likely escaped Nazis themselves. After all, it was hardly necessary to hide their loyalties amongst so many apparent Nazis and Nazi sympathizers.

"One of the men who arrived in Buenos Aires in 1947 is the Swedish Nazi and SS volunteer Hans-Caspar Krueger. He's employed as an instructor in the Argentinean army, and has become a linchpin to assist Nazi escape plans using the same address on Suipacha for a small travel agency. Have any guesses who his clientele is?" asked Mrs. Ernst. "That address is a center for the flow of Aryan fugitives from Europe who would surely have faced death, torture or imprisonment if they had been found after Hitler's death in their Nazi homelands."

Mamma, when given this information, displayed consternation and asked, "With no evidence of sanity in our present political climate, how do we keep paranoia from overriding reason? I have always believed in universal truths, even while being surrounded by global lies. How many of these lies are deadly lies? Will we again experience political imprisonment, loss of free speech, intolerance of differing opinions, oppression by our government? With emotions in the very blood coursing through my veins furiously, I will not allow fear to pervade our lives again. Fear can make cowards of us all."

Dr. Ernst cleared his throat conspicuously and motioned for us to take seats. The reports were to begin. "I find most people around us have a circumscribed, or restrictive, world view. I trust our research, reporting and conclusions will take us beyond that, as good investigative journalism will do. Life doesn't wait for fools. It pushes them to stagger along the road called idiocy. Let the education begin!"

TWENTY-SIX

January 15, 1949

HOPE AND FEAR

Walter Leones dropped the -ski from his family name after fleeing Occupied Poland in 1942. Most customers experienced the terse shop owner of Luca's Bookstore as knowledgeable, friendly and unobtrusive. Between those qualities and the brilliance of Luca herself, the business was a thriving presence in Nuevo Cordoba, home to universities. Situated in Los Altos del Sur, those higher lands to the south of Cordoba's downtown, Nuevo Cordoba's relationship to downtown and Parque Sarmiento at the city's heart, appealed to the high class of Cordoba who built their houses there, many of which over time were replaced by modern apartment buildings, housing thousands of students. Interestingly, buildings closest to downtown were those Italian builders had constructed for prosperous businessmen, themselves descendants of immigrants! The higher landforms near the University campus College of Agriculture, experienced huge population growth after 1940. The University of Cordoba, founded by Jesuits in 1613, has since characterized Cordoba as the City of Students.

Walter rarely took part in our backroom meetings, but he chose this night in mid-January 1949 to be a "presenter". It was no surprise to us when he began by pulling a straight back wooden chair into our circle and saying, "I have left leanings. I despise authoritarianism, imperialism, ignorance and lies, and I am a marked man. Yes, I am a target of the Nazis, should they ever discover my identity here in Cordoba, but I will back down to no one. I've been accused of being a Nazi sympathizer and traitor to my people, as a consequence of the Nazis taking over my printing press and newspaper production business and forcing me to print and distribute their propagandized material. When they first captured and held my parents and my wife, I was too afraid for their lives to disobey. Were you aware many Poles helped hide Jews? Over six million Poles perished, one in five! I feared, I grieved, and we fled, but first I regularly subverted their lying propaganda by hiding messages in advertisements exposing Nazi plans, locations and lies. The underground resistance knew well where to look to decode messages I passed on regularly to aid their efforts. Best of all, I destroyed the entire printing press the day my wife, Caterine and her parents were killed in the bombs planted along the Warsaw Ghetto fence. Luca and I escaped by assistance from the Swedes, only because my mother's family is Swedish, and their remaining relatives retained hope we might all escape. When they learned of the horrors that befell our family, they sent an infiltrator to bring us to safety."

Luca teared up, looked away from her dad, and grabbed onto the hand extended to hers by Nico. He gently stroked her hand repeatedly as Walter continued. She continued to weep. We took a break, offered her and Walter condolences, comfort and tears of our own, before he resolutely continued.

"World War II brought more suffering to humanity than any other event in the 20th century. Casualties included nearly 60 million people who died throughout six years of war, which saw atomic bombs, cities flattened, civilians fire-bombed, and the Holocaust. Out of the war sprang the atomic age, Cold War and the division of Germany. The war reparations imposed on Germany and Italy can never be repaid, thus serve to humiliate and threaten the former axis members by their victors."

He continued reading, "Looming over all political arenas was the very real threat of communism. You are all aware of these events and consequences. My research report will uncover underlying political philosophies which have resulted, the substance of our uncertain times. You see, when Poland signed the capitulation act on 10 June 1939, the world stood still before the startling and demonic military might of the Third Reich. As one of their earliest acts, the occupying Nazis forced me to operate a propaganda machine churning out the lies propagated by Josef Goebbels, Hitler and his ilk, proving firsthand that people unwittingly believe lies of despots. Lies which are fundamental to the cancerous growth of authoritarian regimes. If you tell a lie several times, it becomes a fact, according to Goebbels. And people desperate for sustenance, security and even national pride want these 'facts' to be true!"

"Democracy, prone to act at a sluggish pace, had not brought the promises of equitable wealth distribution, unionization of workers, banking reforms and anti-corruption. What choice was there then, but to buy into promises of the Communist Party? We are entering a new global contest -- Post-War to Cold War, now the headlines and topic of many conversations. I can't keep enough pamphlets and books on these topics on my shelves."

I broke in, asking about the Soviets and undercurrents of their relationship with the United States, this 'cold war'. I realized how naive I was, having been caught up in so many other interests, mostly involving my Leica and photojournalism, which I pursued passionately, even distracting me from participating in our family discussions. I rarely read as extensively as I had customarily for as long as I could recall.

Walter appreciated my interest and clarified my concerns for all of us with this wrap-up, "The Red army liberated Eastern Europe from Fascism, and tried to obliterate Nazism as well. All war crimes were blamed on the Nazis. The Soviets offered a 'new order' to encompass the working class and offer impoverished people a hope -- a hope Western Democracy had spoken of, emptily it seems. Extremes are what keep the middle purposeful. The peril was Social Democrats, Christian Democrats and anything Liberal would be suspect, weak and then be easily overtaken by the Communist Party. Anti-Fascism should be fierce, irreversible and rewarded! Democratic oversight in this light, seemed grossly insufficient. The brutality of war has led to a 'cold war', producing a menacing peace."

Dr. Ernst stiffened and muttered aloud, "Peace? The chaotic, repressed, under-educated populace of this planet know *no* peace -- not now and not into eternity! Better to work to achieve harmony and respect. What is peace anyway?"

That candid outburst seemed to provide impetus for others to speak up and produced disagreements alongside varying levels of conversation. Walter admitted to shortening the paper by leaving out more detailed information he would provide to anyone of us, at our request.

Walter's final commentary centered on class struggle. "Nearly all Westernized nations were polarized by the political tug-of-war resulting from Post-War restlessness and unease. Some joined the Communists, in betrayal of Social Democratic modalities of "class struggle". With these serious divisions, will the greater need for ridding the planet of Nazis and ensuring an end to Fascism be under-represented in the principal movements sweeping over the world, as threats to peace? I tell you, no nation is now isolated either in war or in peace. Every authoritarian and totalitarian regime in history has eventually failed, and if we remain diligent, cannot again take stronghold, except when the people are uneducated. Never underestimate the power of the uninformed voters to choose wrongly and welcome in tyranny."

TWENTY-SEVEN

PROTECTING FREEDOM
FROM THE LIES

Papa waited for Walter's final comments and then mentioned to us his own world observation, i.e., discontents become malcontents. "Discontent is so not the same as greed. Greed can be satisfied; discontent just seethes and feeds on itself. Discontent manifests in claws; greed in jaws! Greed demands more; discontent holds within its bowels constant insatiable hungers. One is excessive desire, the other compulsive vengeful rage. Greed has been seen wearing a pretty face; discontent cannot masquerade. Greed stifles; discontent incites."

Those statements were startlingly incisive enough that many of us entered them in our notes word-for-word. In the side bar of my notepaper I added, "So then, how must we oppose war and make post-war policies to create a liberal world order?"

Papa chose to follow with information he prepared on the Marshall Plan. "I hardly need to convince anyone here that U.S. General George Marshall, Secretary of State under President Harry Truman, keenly aware of those factors, made it nearly a holy mission to send American aid to the European countries which had endured the greatest damages. It was their populations that needed to witness renewal, hope and opportunity for rebuilding. Twentieth century American presidents are exceptional at recovery efforts -- look at the New Deal! Notably, Mussolini owned the press, so coverage of Roosevelt's programs was rarely presented. The Italians, had they known, could have used his successful programs as templates for their own recovery efforts. Instead, *Il Duce* subverted all the state could have accomplished to his own objectives!" he commented bitterly.

Papa returned to his written report, "As United States Secretary of State, George C. Marshall devised a plan. In his radio address to the U.S. following his commencement speech at Harvard University in May 1947, he stated '...the recovery of Europe has been far slower than had been expected. Disintegrating forces are becoming evident. The patient is sinking while the doctors deliberate...action cannot await compromise through exhaustion.' Secretary Dean Acheson emphatically stated 'Only two great powers remained in the world, the U.S. and the Soviet Union...And it was clear that the Soviet Union was aggressive and expanding. For the U.S. to take steps to strengthen countries threatened with Soviet aggression...was to protect not only the security of the United States -- it was to protect freedom itself...' What was at stake, then was nothing less than the very survival of Western civilization itself."

"Millions of Europeans were dead or displaced. Many immigrated to North and South America. During six years of World War II thousands of cities and towns across Europe and Asia were destroyed. World Capitals such as Berlin, Tokyo, Warsaw, Manila and Peking were left in ruins. Jews who had survived the holocaust began flooding into Palestine to establish a Jewish state. Israel's statehood, hard won in 1947, is now leading to a series of likely major wars in the Middle East."

"To obtain the generous aid the United States would be willing to make available, those European countries which had endured the most serious devastation of the war followed by devastating weather conditions of 1946 -- drought and nearly unprecedented blizzards-- must collaborate their individual requests and collectively petition aid addressing their specific recovery needs. The

U.S. State Department mandated to Italy and France, to attain aid they must purge the Communists out of their cabinets. Under the Marshall Plan, the United States would provide more than $16 billion in loans, supplies and technical assistance to 16 countries between 1948 and 1951 (except to Spain, still fighting a civil war and under General Franco's dictatorship). In order to receive this funding, each country had to agree to set liberal, capitalist economic policies and expand trade with other European countries."

"Your history books are too skimpy, leaving out most of the details, leaving out all the character necessary to achieve stability through the comprehensive maneuverings of Marshall and Truman, providing economic aid and political strictures. Marshall had to endure seemingly endless sessions with his Soviet equivalent, Foreign Minister Molotov, whose participation in these talks was meant to assure the Soviets would have dominion over Germany, its archenemy. Imagine what it has been like for defeated Germany to be the center of strife over war reparations and its dismemberment amongst the Soviets, France, the U.S. and Britain."

"Also overlooked but very significant was what I call the other issue, Stalin's recollection that at the Yalta conference 2 years prior, the Soviets would receive $10 billion dollars in war reparations over ten years. The Soviets were steadfast, obdurate and bullying, as was expected. They did not get a chance at the foreign aid meted out to Western European countries. In signing the plan, officially called the Economic Recovery Program, Truman declared, 'This measure is America's answer to the challenge facing the free world.' The Western European economy improves greatly, as food cultivation, manufacturing production, employment rates and trade all increase."

"My family is aware that I can be long winded and even, God help me, bombastic. I will conclude by asking you to also ponder a question which has often plagued me. Taking a global-historical perspective, could a non-punitive, constructive policy ending WWI have established a functionally effective League of Nations? And what will be forthcoming consequences of hideous atrocities, many only uncovered as the Allies liberated the Concentration Camps? Juli's question haunts me as I also consider, will those consequences of atrocities in our lifetime be carried in our genes?" Papa adjusted his seat and looked more exhausted than usual as he waved away the offer of iced tea.

Dr. Ernst spoke next, without benefit of notes. "In Buenos Aires, there is a neighborhood housing Nazi elite and their active propaganda machine, *Der Weg,* whose editorial office is at 156, Suilpacha, on the same street as the Swedish Embassy. There's no notice on the door of this ordinary house in the well-to-do part of town. This monthly magazine is a link for the Nazis of Latin America with their counterparts in Europe including tens of thousands of Germans. I've heard the magazine's collaborators are made to feel welcome in the Argentinian president's palace. President Perón himself has instructed a zealot young German-Argentinean to recruit a thousand highly educated people with Aryan blood to come to Argentina. This Carlos Schultz, a patient of mine, has obtained long lists of Nazis in Sweden, and other northern refugees who are known to have worked for the Nazis. When he receives their names, his local links provide exit visas and authorization to enter the country. Passports are stolen and forged, identities are concealed, and Nazis who have been in hiding or on the run are escorted to freedom along the 'rat lines' to a *welcoming* Argentina."

"Before I proceed, I feel tension in the room, suggesting questions. I'll be glad to elucidate, both with information of which I am mostly certain and with the pieces of supposed facts of which I hope to learn more." Dr. Ernst then called on our cousin Matteo who mentioned he could confirm some of the information about *Der Weg* and its editor Eberhard Fritsch, as his older sister, Silvia has been dating a Nazi sympathizer. "We all despise that she is associating with him, yet we're fortunate he has been trying to win her over to his side by sharing his dark German Nazi voice with her. He's asked her to accompany him to meetings, but she declines, always stating she is not German speaking and couldn't be engaged in conversations amongst his friends. She's learned though, the paper and the meeting attendees have been denying Nazi genocide."

Matteo continued, his voice rising, "In the meat packing plant where my Papa and Tio Carmine are in management positions, is a German line worker who emigrated with his family last year. He is overwhelmingly ashamed of everything committed under the Third Reich's policy of Lebensraum, living space, and war crimes of which he is now aware. He's dedicated to ridding all remnants of Nazism but admits to living in trepidation there could be recriminations against his wife and five children."

Mamma turned towards Matteo and asked, "Could that be Phillip, whose wife Valeria I've been having for lunch and helping find clothing for her children?" Matteo affirmed it was Phillip, but begged Mamma not to pass this information on to anyone.

"Now I'm reflecting on a nagging suspicion which is shared by both Julietta and myself. Aboard the Vulcania during our ocean crossing, another German family, befriended us since we were -- not coincidentally -- made dinner companions in the "Azure Seas' group." That drew a few laughs and some curious expressions, as Mamma continued. "The Weiss family, veritably following us to Cordoba, has continued to try to be close acquaintances with us, although we have little in common, and I've recently invited them to our home. Are they tracking us for some sinister reason? I'm aware that the Monsignor from our parish had something to do with the intentional placing of that family in our group aboard the ship. I think I should be concerned about their many queries, perhaps not so innocent, that I answered. How do I find out if there's some kind of plot involving my family? My brother Fabio suggested they may be double agents, befriending us, but for -- what?"

Brenda Ernst leaned towards Mamma and whispered, "Maybe I can drop by during your dinner and play dumb. Two heads are better than one. What time is the dinner?" Mamma jotted down the time and names Albert and Marta Weiss, firming up the tacit agreement.

Chachio asked to be allowed to speak a few words before concluding so all might have time to consider these findings before *trying* to sleep tonight. He can be off-hand and even goofy, so we expected something like a quote he'd used in a similar context, from his favorite writer, Mark Twain, "It's easier to fool people than to convince them that they have been fooled." Instead, he ended with this reminder, "Take heart and stand by our rights, as enthroned into our hopes and dreams by the late President FDR: There are four universal Freedoms: Freedom of speech, Freedom of religion, Freedom from fear, and Freedom from misery. Take heart!"

"My topic for the next meeting will be furthering Mr. Migliore's question about building a societal infrastructure to assure constitutional and legal rights to the people. We **will** resist authoritarianism, and I will outline the means to do so." Chachio took an exaggerated bow and said, "Don't be so surprised!"

Walter and Luca opened the back door for us to exit, reminding us we should arrive earlier for the next meeting on 31 January, as they have ordered some survivalist and activist handbooks we might want to purchase, and definitely to remain unobtrusive but ever watchful, as we prepare for the rest of the reporting. What was he referring to?

TWENTY-EIGHT

---◆○◆---

31 January 1949

THE ROOTS OF EVIL

Everyone who attended the last meeting at the Revolutionary Bookstore arrived early as instructed. Walter passed out booklets which had just arrived and asked us to pay for them next week, after our reading, suggesting we prepare comments for that meeting. He passed out mimeographed copies of an article he found in the New York Times, and asked us to read this recent piece. "The Times has the best journalism and writing. I know it is not easy to read the material in English, but the Spanish language version available here just doesn't have the exact same coverage and it arrives a week later than the publishing date in New York. Luca can translate, if needed, for this article:

"J. Edgar Hoover, director of the FBI, stated, "The Communist Party...has for its purpose the shackling of America and its conversion to the Godless, Communist way of life... We, of this generation, have faced two great menaces...Fascism and Communism. Both are materialistic; both are totalitarian; both are anti-religious; both are degrading and inhuman."

"Soviet domination might ...extend over the entire Middle East to the borders of India" declared Dean Acheson. The domino theory of one nation falling might cause the next and so on. "It is not alarmist to say that we are faced with the first crisis of a series which might extend Soviet domination to Europe, the Middle East and Asia."

"These were his arguments for aid initially meant for Greece and Turkey, when Great Britain declared they could no longer send aid to either of their former dominions." Walter said, clearing his throat and taking sips of iced tea.

Reading further, "The Marshall Plan was necessitated by the devastation of World War II in Europe and the emerging U.S. foreign policy of containment. European countries suffered widespread hunger and high levels of unemployment, which made their governments vulnerable to upheaval. The Truman administration, fearing that Soviet communism would spread to the West, hoped to combat and contain it by helping to rebuild European economies. ... Sixteen European nations met in Paris over the summer to negotiate how to organize the acceptance of U.S. aid. The Soviet Union and five Eastern Bloc countries refused to take part and thus would not receive Marshall Plan funding."

Walter reminded us while we are Catholics, we may not agree with alarmists denouncing communism as the great godless threat, and many of the anti-Fascists who fought hardest and bravest were the Partisans, most of whom proclaimed to be avowed communists, though he knew many of them still prayed. "Religious freedom is a liberty worth fighting for, is it not? I think the Communist creed forbids religious affiliation because of its dubious opposition to "the ends justify the means", although Stalin has seemed more than willing to use *any* means to obtain his desired ends". With that he turned over the floor to Chachio.

"I wish to offer accolades to those brave men and women of the resistance who sacrificed everything in the name of freedom. In their honor, I made this report about the roots of Fascism and steps to resist authoritarianism. If I'm being fully candid, I wrote this for a term paper, and towards my application to the Honor Society of the Law

School, careful not to mention the current dictator who calls himself our president of Argentina."

The Roots of Fascism

1. Extreme nationalism

2. Disdain for human rights

3. Enemies are named and become scapegoats as a unifying cause

4. Supremacy of the military

5. Sexism and despising of homosexuality

6. State control of mass media

7. Obsession with national security

8. Government controlled religion

9. Protection of corporate power

10. Suppression of labor movements

11. Disdain for intellectuals, artists and teachers who do not serve their causes

12. Obsession with criminality and excessive punishment

13. Rampant corruption and "You scratch my back and I'll scratch yours"

14. Fraudulent elections

15. Revolution is never from the masses, but from the top down

16. Anti-liberal, anti-communist and anti-socialist pronounced agendas

17. Extreme exploitation

18. Destructive and intentional divisiveness

19. Opportunistic ideologies

20. Use of crushing violence and terror

21. Cult-like figureheads

22. Censorship, propaganda, denouncement of facts and truths

"Maybe that doesn't cover all aspects of these dictatorships which thrive on propagandized ideology and their version of justice. These regimes have no trace of justice or decency, for they embrace power at all costs." At this, Chachio lifted his head and received a sound reverberating ovation from us. Walter put his finger to his lips to remind us to keep the volume down. These are secret meetings, we must remember.

With a flourish, Chachio continued, "Recognition of these phenomena is the first step, refusing to believe the lies inherent in them is the next. The masses must be won by propaganda and blind faith. Beliefs can be corrupted. Remember the Roman Caesars and senators who blindsided the populace with bread and circuses. Sounds like Mussolini's tactics, doesn't it?"

Yes, we nodded assent. After all, he'd been summing up tyranny and putting a spotlight on one particular despot, the very one who still produced a vile taste in our mouths just to speak or hear his name!

"The masses, as long as they remain ignorant, remain powerless against those who use the tools of the authoritarian to manipulate minds and sway public opinion to distorted reality as they direct it. Before long propaganda myths are not illusory, but motivating to the despot's ends of imperialism, war, and military and constitutional control. Awareness is the first step, followed by resolutely refusing to believe, and refusing to allow the lies to be spread. The people have power of the vote and unionization to demand their rights, or despots will ultimately control education, the press and all forms of speech."

"As I said, in a climate of chaos, uncertainty, fear and divisiveness, a 'savior' will arise, promising, as Hitler, Mussolini and Perón, order and prosperity will be restored as soon as he is leader and there is one party. Anyone not loyal to that party will suffer terrible consequences and put their livelihood and family at risk. Recognize next, we will be made to be suspicious of each other, fearing to be turned in as subversives and traitors or to be found out as one of the state's declared enemies."

"Before the leader becomes a despotic tyrant, we must hold firm to our principles and our values. They must be reinforced in the culture at large through education, public speaking out, protests, an unwavering free press, and resistance to divisiveness. Constant vigilance and bravery are required. Our power as a people demands we do not relinquish our power as an individual. Thank you, John Locke. The politicians have eyes and ears, and will use the very words of a dissatisfied populace to create assurances the voters' demands will be met, *by them only*. We must and will see through those fractured lenses of politics to place power ***only*** in the hands of those who have shown they have earned our trust and will honor it."

Luca got up and hugged Chachio, saying, "I knew you had it in you! I'd like to type that on mimeograph and print it for all of us -- and pass it out tomorrow, to be a discussion point in our classes as well. Bravo!"

Chachio, moving to his seat, asked Luca to refrain from signing his name to the report which he would be glad to distribute widely and anonymously.

TWENTY-NINE

1 February 1949

THE HOLY INFANT'S SECRET

I set the table and helped Mamma prepare the meal for the Weiss family the next evening. Nico had not arrived yet, and Papa had yet to be dropped off by Tio Paolo when the Weiss family arrived promptly at 19:00. It was quite warm so there were no wraps to gather. Marta gave Mamma and I air kisses to each cheek and remarked on the pervasive charm she felt from the welcome message on the door to the loveliness of the home itself. "You have an altar, just like mine and some I've seen in the homes of devout friends in Italy. Has this blessed Infant of Prague been in your family for generations? Mine was gifted to me from my aunt, who lovingly made four robes for it. What does the white robe he is wearing represent?"

Mamma replied, smoothly deceptive, "We are between the season of Nativity celebrated last month when the child Jesus wore a red robe, and the holy season of lent, which garment is purple, then Easter which is green." I was aware she was intentionally misleading Marta, as all Catholics know the Ecclesiastical colors are symbolically, white for Christmas and Easter, purple for lent, and red for Holy Week. We used the blue robe for special family occasions, especially wedding anniversaries. "Do you continue this tradition, Marta?"

"I have, until I had to leave the statue behind. So much stuff to pack into the trunks! But my aunt and parents assured me they will bring it when they visit." Marta responded, and added, "My mother prays in front of our altar daily for my brother, who hasn't been heard from since he was found to have subversive materials at an underground raid in 1942. He had just turned 16 and didn't want to participate in Hitler's war."

I pivoted by asking Mamma to check on the cooking with me. We closed the double doors leading from the living room to the kitchen and I blurted out, "If she has a brother in peril or missing, why has she not mentioned that before? And as for her devotion to the Christ child, she managed to take trunk loads of toys and clothes with them, but not a treasured gift, like the statue of our dear Infant?"

"Julietta, she is a fraud! I took your advice and have been planting misleading comments to test her genuineness. She's failed on each account. Mrs. Ernst will be 'dropping by' when she takes Nico home within the hour, after dinner. I'll invite her to meet Marta and Albert and have dessert with us. She and I have our own trap planned to circumspectly watch and catch whichever one of them has been tracking us. We still don't know what they expect us to possess, but Brenda suggested we may have something the Nazi escape network wants to recover, almost certainly stolen wealth to support the Aryan Nazi fugitives from Germany."

We returned to our company and while Mamma showed them our house and vegetable garden, I prepared my camera so I could catch on film any actions which might give away Marta and Albert's plan. Papa arrived in time to sit down with us to dinner and while raising his wine glass, proposed this prayer as a toast, "Heavenly Father, who has brought us together in our new country, please prepare us to enjoy this meal and companionship. In the light of Your love. Amen." We all lifted our wine glasses and passed the beef and potatoes baked with peppers and onions, just taken from the oven, imparting a fragrance so dreamy you could almost drink it! As we enjoyed the dinner, Marta and Albert talked at length about their children, new home, new job and even some political references, obliquely referring to unsavory Perónist tactics.

Marta and Mamma got up to clear the table and dishes, while I set out chilled chocolate chip cannolis and fresh orange slices. Before I could pour the almond liqueur, Mrs. Ernst and Nico arrived, so I included them as Mamma made introductions. If it wasn't an auspicious evening, anyone might have thought this was a lovely, friendly dinner, until Marta excused herself, asking for a moment to read over the short letter from her mother which she hadn't had time to read before setting out for our dinner. "Albert is all about punctuality, so I had to set the letter in my handbag, but I simply want a few minutes to glance over and hopefully set my mind at ease."

She walked into the living room, closing the doors behind her, leaving an awkward silence. Brenda and Mamma exchanged glances as Albert knocked over his wine glass and its contents spilled onto Nico and the floor. Perfect diversion for them, perfect opportunity for us, allowing Brenda to slip completely unnoticed into the living room where she swooped up her camera and snapped a picture of Marta, whose both hands grasped the Infant of Prague. The flash scared Mrs. Weiss who turned to Mrs. Ernst and angrily accused her of nearly causing the statue to crash. "I was in prayer, supplicating Christ to help my brother and my distraught parents! How dare you intrude?"

Mamma entered, stood next to Brenda and glared at Marta as she asked, "Why exactly are you holding my statue? Praying is a veiled excuse, my friend! You are seeking something, so what and where is it?"

By now everyone was witnessing this scene as Mr. Weiss staunchly demanded Marta set the statue back and say goodnight. Marta grabbed her handbag and whipped it at my camera as I was taking a photo of her, knocking it to our hardwood floor and shrieking, "I trusted you and you have treated me like I, myself, am the untrustworthy one! It's a betrayal to our mutual friendship to accuse me of motives and actions of which I know nothing. I am innocent!"

Papa directed this notice to them, "Well, *innocenti*, it shouldn't surprise you we are too vigilant for your bullshit!"

They walked out without any further comments, closing the door in the same staunch manner Albert used when he forced her away. Not having been given any answers, Brenda and Mamma placed the now suspect statue on the coffee table to examine for themselves what it must be hiding.

"My camera!" I carefully lifted and examined it, noting with utter dismay the viewfinder lens had cracked. Through a fountain of tears, I handed it to Mrs. Ernst who examined it and reassured me the other lenses seemed intact, and those were the ones which would be necessary to take a photograph. The viewfinder could still provide a focal perspective, surely affecting the subject as I might see it, but not the quality of the photograph. She suggested I finish the roll now, and she would have it developed first thing tomorrow, a rush job, so I could be reassured it was fully functional.

I shot more photos, as everyone convened, discussing what might have been happening, and I stood by to photograph what mystery could be found in the statue. "Do we all recall Monsignor taking this statue to be blessed, and sincerely admonishing us to make it the centerpiece of our new lives in Cordoba? We spoke about the steward's report of Monsignor, covertly bringing the Weiss family together with us on our voyage." I pondered, still upset.

Mamma went a step further adding, "Brenda, I told you some of this and you advised me to be suspicious. Thank you for coming tonight and standing firm against Marta's pathetic excuses."

Papa held the statue and examined it very closely, shook it, and asked for a safety pin so he could poke and pry at the orb where he thought he'd heard something rattle. He carefully removed the robes as Brenda handed him a hatpin, stuck into the lining of her handbag. It proved to be thick and firm enough for him to prod, finally hitting upon a hidden hinge. Now popped open, the orb revealed a small sack of silk wrapping, which Mamma carefully grasped, placing it into the palm of her left hand while exploring the contents with her right. Mrs. Ernst snapped a photo of the deep green emerald drop surrounded by filigreed gold. Six rubies and multiple small diamonds were inset around the oval emerald, on a glimmering gold chain. She let out a gasp, "These are amongst the gems stolen from an Austrian Jewish industrialist family who fled for their lives as Nazis occupied their country. In Berlin, I had seen a flyer showing this piece and several other custom creations plundered from their collection. I stand here in utter amazement, thinking this cannot be!"

I spoke next, "But it can be, as it found its way from the Nazis to the Church, to be stashed for safe passage on unsuspecting carriers. We are just that -- innocent of wrongdoing while guilty of being unwitting accomplices. We could have been killed in the retrieval attempt, especially one that has been thwarted, and it would have been more blood on the hands of the Vatican, and of Monsignor!"

Mamma spoke what we all had been thinking, "What do we do with this and the knowledge of how it was placed there?" She passed the lightweight, highly valued piece to Brenda who took several photographs of it, then passed it to Papa so we could all take a closer look at the treasure, saying: "I will bring my loupe here in the morning, but I am already certain of the authenticity of this necklace. So delicately wrought, with perfect gems befitting the neckline of an empress. It should be returned to the rightful owners' heirs, perhaps through the War Crimes Commission, so they can track down the chain of crimes from its theft to the attempt to recapture the stolen gems."

Mamma and Papa nodded agreement. Nico paced back and forth, then asked Papa to keep his pistol loaded and ready in case another attempt is made. "Albert or Marta may make another even bolder attempt by breaking in while they believe the house is empty, or they may be directed to engage another perpetrator. We are in danger as long as this in our possession, even at this moment. While we prepare a plan of action, I'd like to take Mamma tomorrow to lease a safe deposit box to keep it from any possible further theft attempts."

Mrs. Ernst's next suggestion was straight out of a spy novel. "I can reproduce this piece and re-plant the fake inside the orb as if we had never recovered it. There will be other attempts to steal this from its sacred storage in your home, but it might be years or days from now. May I suggest you confer with your brother, Angelina, and nobody else. We want your Nazi-loving Monsignor Oliverio to believe you're clueless about the jewels and innocent of the part Marta and Albert had been set up for. We can set up a trap of our own, once Fabio and the War Crimes Commission have been brought into the loop. Let's sleep on it tonight and be sure to lock up your doors and windows!"

Difficult would be an understatement to describe re-composing our lives; can such a small adjective encompass what we tell the members of our groups -- school, volunteer organizations, workplace, relatives, and mainly the several of us who met to elucidate the political climate here in Argentina in early 1949? Mamma spoke very briefly to Fabio, only able to tell him Monsignor had set our family up in a betrayal and theft scheme, before he broke in, advising her to keep everything quiet while he proceeded to dig deeper into the Genovese clerics and suspected Nazi escape network which brought war criminals and hordes of treasures stolen from the Jews and occupied nations into Argentina. Tio Fabio was on a mission, secret as usual, and asked us to hang tight (a parachutist's terminology?) until next week when Mamma could tell him the entire story.

Papa reminded us, raising his arms to shoulder level, palms towards him, an Italian fact of life is summed up, *'Nulla è mai stato risolto,'* 'nothing is ever resolved," but none of us found that funny. Enlightening and true, at least in my experience, but not reassuring. We all agreed we'd carry on with our assignments and questions for the group meetings at Luca's bookstore, but we wouldn't reveal this event until we had spoken to Fabio. Mrs. Ernst and Mamma carried on a daily communication, sharing updates from Alfred and the doctor. I learned they also shared their past grief over miscarriages which would have borne welcomed children. Sorrow shared is sorrow halved, and who better to share with than one who has suffered the same type of loss?

THIRTY

◆○◆

SAFE PASSAGE FOR RATS

The dissident dozen. That's an apt description of the group that came together at Luca's bookstore the evening of 7 February 1949. The small room was stifling with the number of bodies, amongst them regulars and again including guest members, Dr. and Mrs. Ernst and my parents. Yes, this would be extraordinary and memorable. After acknowledging our honored speakers for this evening, Luca asked her father to please close the store and take notes while attending this presentation.

Everyone had been preparing their evidence, conjectures, and conclusions, sometimes spurious, but taken together, they provided remarkable clarity. The secure passage which enabled elite Nazis safe entry into South American countries, specifically to Argentina, was real, identifiable, and called "the rat line", or "ODESSA", a German acronym for Organization of Former Members of the SS. The parents present were exceptionally well informed, educated and notably alarmed enough to risk being caught collecting this information, and now laying out a scheme which would be a call to action. This was no usual meeting for discourse.

The fireball started the meeting with all eyes on her. Luca was outgoing, inclusive, creative, and brilliant. As co-owner and manager of Luca's Books, which we all spoke amongst each other as Revolution in Books (Revolucion en Los Libros or R.E.L.L.) she was also a writer for some University periodicals and had an interview published in an Argentinean magazine!

"*Gratias* to each of you who have researched, analyzed and will now report on aspects of Nazi escape routes. You are enormously brave witnesses turned activists. You are immigrants like my father and me, who could not endure brutal authoritarian regimes destroying our European homes. Most of us left Nazi and Fascist regimes, arriving in Argentina to learn its President Perón is himself a fascist populist. Clearly, we have departed from a turbulent Europe to a fomenting turbulence in Argentina." Luca poured her prepared iced tea and invited us to enjoy the lovely oval shaped, powdered sugar-dusted cruschiki cookies, a freshly baked gift to Walter, who, at great difficulty, provided literature for a widowed immigrant baker in her native Polish tongue.

"We don't have a round table, nor any table at all since this backroom accommodates stacks of books and only has room for our few chairs. This evening's discussions will begin after the researched materials and information have been presented, and we'll start with the very person who asked we initiate this investigation, Mrs. Brenda Ernst."

"I am honored that you students, deserving of much admiration and needing much security (some laughs burst out from the group), have asked the Migliore's and ourselves to participate and contribute our considerable information and perspectives. I'll do my best now and in any future endeavors for which I can move this investigation forward." She then read her findings.

"Escape organizations on an incredible scale existed all over Europe following the war, even from late 1944 when it was becoming clear Germany would not be the victor in this war. And what would happen to the vanquished murderers, the Nazi elite? They were all expecting biased trials and immediate executions as they, themselves would have done, minus the trials of course. We had read and been 'assured' there was not a singular organization founded and financed by SS agents early in the war. Instead, it seems small groups of individuals created networks out of necessity once they found themselves suddenly on the wrong side of history. Their motivations were to help themselves and fellow Nazis find a way to continue their lives without fear and without having to answer for their involvement in Nazi war crimes. Argentina became this beacon of hope. The Perón government could provide stability and comfort European countries could not."

"There are now many living amongst us throughout South America who are notorious, wanted war criminals. Angelina's report has provided details and conclusions we must take seriously, along with everything we can piece together from our reports. Even 'conjecture' must be considered."

"On October 20, 1945, the International Military Tribunal took its seat at the Nuremberg Palace of Justice. What has become known as the Nuremberg trial was the first of 13 trials held there. Twenty-four high-ranking Nazi leaders were charged with crimes against peace, war crimes, and crimes against humanity. They stood accused of murder, extermination, enslavement, deportation and persecution on political, racial, or religious grounds, and conspiracy to commit these crimes. My brother, Professor Alfred Reicher, has been in frequent communication with me from his home in New York City, and his shocking revelations — accusations with considerable evidence — should alarm all of us. They are based on media reports and lawsuits coming from the United States and England."

"Alfred wrote recently, 'Never before had crimes committed by a state been brought before a court of law, never before had responsibility been established for a nation's acts, and never before had crimes ordered by a head of government been articulated and brought to a courtroom. The chief prosecutor, Robert H. Jackson, an American, proclaimed, as he was wrapping up his case in the proceedings, 'These defendants now ask the tribunal to say they are not guilty of planning, executing or conspiracy to commit this long list of crimes and wrongs.' Jackson had staked his prosecution on the conspiracy theory vs. actual commission of crimes. 'If you were to say of these men that they are not guilty, it would be as true to say that there has been no war, there are no slain, there has been no crime. The neat logic of the prosecution was that individuals conspire to evil intent; they create organizations to achieve their ends; therefore, both the individuals and the organizations are criminal.' Jackson's argument was this was a regime deliberately embarked on war. The trial of war criminals, then must signal not simply the triumph of superior might, but the triumph of superior morality. He hoped this would be a position to assure aggressive warfare would no longer be accepted as another political activity, but dealt with as a crime against humanity, with aggressors treated as criminals. There would be no defense in consideration of Fuëhrerprinzip, the ironbound obedience to the Fuëhrer!"

Walter nodded to Papa to proceed. Papa cleared his throat and began with President Harry S. Truman's formal missive announcing the end of War in Europe:

> "All Fascism did not die with Mussolini. Hitler is finished – but the seeds spread by his disordered mind have firm root in too many fanatical brains. It is easier to remove tyrants and destroy concentration camps than it is to kill the ideas which gave them birth and strength. Victory on the battlefield was essential, but it was not enough. For a good peace, a lasting

peace, the decent peoples of the earth must remain determined to strike down the evil spirit which has hung over the world for the last decade. The forces of reaction and tyranny all over the world will try to keep the United Nations from remaining united. Even while the military machine of the Axis was being destroyed in Europe – even down to its very end – they still tried to divide us.

They failed. But they will try again."

My Papa has re-read President's Truman's message, which my family heard together, in his radio message after the war's end, several times. This time Papa suggested, "The principal movements sweeping over the world were accelerated by the war, but the American president spoke so much truth-in-warning with those statements. Repeating his words, I hope to convince others we should be looking forward through hindsight. I believe by shining a spotlight on our past, we will illuminate the darkness that would otherwise bring fear and hatred to the present."

He added, "Follow the light to expose the truth. That's what my Papa Rosario always said. Don't fight just against what you hate. Fight for what you love. How could these be uniquely Italian ideals? I'm not sure I see these virtues evidenced in other cultures." There were several comments from the group, and in response, or perhaps simply ruminating, Papa questioned, "When is the right time to confront the truth about matters questioning our ideals and matters we should hold in suspicion? Most people seem to live their lives like it's never the right time."

Nico had been thoughtfully listening, nodding and taking notes, before adding his own on post-war confusion.

"Luca's father gave me a bootlegged copy of leaflets produced by The White Rose movement, a cause begun by siblings Hans and Sophie Scholl, allied with fellow University of Munich students. With the publication and distribution, at their great peril, they hoped to commence a movement to end the Nazi regime. They called for passive resistance against Hitler's regime by appealing to German citizens' intellect, intuition and sense of shame. SHAME for standing by silently as atrocities were committed; SHAME for their supporting the propagandist government's lying assertions towards the Jewish race, for allowing so many to be senselessly murdered and for allowing their country to be overtaken by fascism through fear. Where was the moral outrage necessary for action?" Nico stopped and returned to the question of moral justice.

"The White Rose movement existed to incite the German people to act out against the Nazi government, to save their country from a legacy of disgrace. The six core members were executed for high treason, injuring the war potential of the Reich, and more. They *were* a treasonous group -- against a government committing treason against humanity -- making the White Rose members noble. Papa, you had a book on governance by John Locke, who invoked the right of the people to revolt against a government which fails to preserve the lives and property of its citizens. Nazi laws disregarded the sanctity of human life. They had only contempt for the Declaration of Independence' words, 'it is the right and the duty of the people...to alter or abolish...' unjust laws and governments."

All eyes turned to Papa when he said, "Nico, I have always known you understand why I fought in resistance maneuvers against the Germans and any remaining pro-

Fascist military. I fought to eliminate Fascism which stifles personal growth and expression and demands citizens live to serve the state. Like Communists, they work toward destruction of all forms of personal independence, whether economic, political or moral. These elements are growing here in Argentina, where I hear Perón supporters, including the mass of workers, are called Pero-Nazis. Maybe that is unjust, and if discovered could be political suicide. I fear the turning to authoritarian populism throughout the world, as long as despots are supported by a propaganda machine and the populace averts their eyes and subverts their conscience. Moral justice requires acts of heroism, not allowed under tyranny!"

"The Peace Agreement ending the war in Europe left suffering Europeans in dark desperation, polarizing the provocateurs -- the Axis members -- to seek relief. We had a choice when the 1946 Italian referendum created a Republic and eliminated the monarchy, right? Social Democrats appealed to industrialists and middle class, while Communists promised labor unionization, better wages and eventually ownership over means of production. Damn right, that appealed to the masses! Italians were still in bitter poverty and chaos as they voted largely for the Communist party. Were we losers in *every* regard? The Allies forced war reparations on Germany and on us, the conquered ones. Should anyone be surprised despair and hopelessness would prevail?"

Papa may have been long-winded, but his passionate and knowledgeable commentary was well received. Without putting words to it, we considered him a war hero, truly brave and a voice, even a conscience for us.

I began by asking Walter and Luca if they could provide some "How to" literature, like "How to Be: An Anti-Fascist", "How to Be A Resistance Fighter", "How to be An Activist/Spy/Counterspy..." "Add to that list, "How to survive: major famines, all the -isms, and an emergency pamphlet offering advice on hiding under fear of death." Sounding more like Frank, rather tongue-in-cheek, these would be worthwhile topics, maybe top sellers if all we are discussing leads to the conclusions we fear are factual. Papa looked at me circumspectly, so I read aloud my topic, "Distorted lenses. Contorted lies!"

Sitting on boxes of inventory for the bookstore, I was unsteady, so I carefully balanced my position and settled myself before speaking. "Clearly, I am the youngest of our group, which I see as an advantage. I bring a fresher, younger perspective to the devastating events we have been discussing and I use my experience of focusing on the picture, as through my camera lens."

"Symbolic of recent events and times in which we live, whatever we view and choose to focus on might be intentionally distorted, even fractured in our seeing, but when that shutter snaps, reality is captured. You can examine a photo again and again, focusing on the greater picture, which is likely to be surprising. Truly surprising."

"This week has been full of revelations, missteps and mishaps. Due to all of that, I needed to make sense of these events and your reports uncovering the complicity of clerics and governments with Nazi elites to create an escape route. Are we being shown alternative realities by media reports, distorting what is actually around us? Like looking through the cracked viewfinder of my camera, I'm more than ever aware of propagandized illusions of our fascist dictatorships. On one hand, we can discuss how they would hide their lying overtures, tyranny and murderous legacy. On the other, I will focus on social democratic ideals, resisting authoritarianism and building a framework, like we learn of in the United States, to assure constitutional and legal rights to the people."

"While other immigrants are assimilated with some assistance from their own nation's benevolent societies established to serve them, these favored Germans receive assistance from a sordid network of Perónists, clerics and former, even active, Nazis to assure *more* than safe passage.

"I'll continue to seek to uncover the truth of what is real in a world of lies and illusions that still shatter the way we see the world today. I believe in universal truths, and I am committed to exposing tyranny's deadly lies. My hope is the stirring optimism of young activists here will also be stirring our parents and teachers. When you experience discontent, that's when you need to turn aside the ideas for revenge and self-destruction and reach for a star."

As I was turning to offer the floor to our final speaker, Frank, I saw tears through smiles on the parents, and nods of agreement from the rest, even Nico. I liked feeling what I spoke really moved the participants in our experimental discussion group.

Frank's self-assurance is always noticeable when he's in the spotlight! He has the bearing of a soldier, the heart of a saint, the charisma of a hero and he's one gorgeous guy besides! "I can't profess to be as scholarly as the rest of you have shown to be, but as final speaker of the night, I prefer to combine our observations and facts into a wrap-up that will expose the deficiencies of autocracy, and reveal openings through which a coalition of informed justice seekers can crush their vile dark intentions, before resorting to violent forms of resistance. Fascists, Nazis, all despots will use unprecedented authority to persecute political enemies. Witness Perón's populist autocracy, mimicking his favorite dictators, Hitler and Mussolini, gathering more might to take down those who write or speak opposition."

"Books are being written and well-respected publications are analyzing events which have changed the world forever. All the parents here know the chronology which started with Hitler's and Mussolini's rise to become "leader" in their respective countries. Oh, the seductive kiss of tyrants! I thank Chachio for his list of the "Roots of Evil" and the rest of you for your input, shedding light on repression and iniquities of the "-isms". Whew! I hope there's no hidden recording device that could be conveying our discussion to the officials."

"It was 25 years ago Hitler fomented the birth of revolution at a beer hall in Munich. With Goering by his side, leading 2000 storm troopers, Hitler declared "The national revolution has begun" and *he* was forming a new government. Shots rang out, the crowd fled for cover, and two days later, Hitler was imprisoned. Just three months later, he went on trial for high treason -- oh, if only the charges had been enough to put an end to him! Instead, he took command of the courtroom, shouting, There is no such thing as high treason against the traitors of 1918, and he would be a future ruler of Germany. A prosecutor asked by what right did he, without education or experience, feel himself worthy of such a position? He replied: A man who is born to be a dictator has a right to step forward. When he was returned to his cell, his comrade Rudolf Hess helped him write <u>Mein Kampf</u>, with its demonic themes." Frank then read some of the most potently vile passages:

"To fight is man's reason for being. A racially pure people can band together and conquer the world through its will. The will of the man at the top is worth more than the votes of a million men. It is not analytical thinking that holds people to the leader, but blind obedience and faith. When I read this to Mr. Migliore, he said it reminded him of the Fascist slogan, '*Credi, combatti e obbedisci*,' 'Believe, fight, and obey."

"The comparison of the two detested dictators goes way beyond: their charismatic bravado, their insistence on total control and total obedience. They employed a time honored tactic of using military, quasi-military and civilians to rout out dissenters, and proceeded to whatever means they chose to remain at the top and dispose of their enemies. In our lifetime, only Stalin may have been worse. I admit I'm a somewhat derelict Catholic, but I know my strength comes from the Divine and I sincerely ask His grace on all of us. The future holds greatness if we refuse to be diminished by despotic power. It's apparent to me from participating in this group, *we* will choose truth over ideology."

"Final words, in this quote from Benjamin Franklin, exiting Philadelphia's Independence Hall where the secret vote of that sundry group of patriots and statesmen was held to decide the form their new government would take. When asked, what form had been decided, Franklin replied, A republic, if you can keep it. Let that remain forefront in our minds and our intentions -- let's fight for that, a free and just republic, and then keep it!"

THIRTY-ONE

••••••◆◇◆••••••

10 February 1949

TO TRAP A THIEF

Considering the magnitude of what had been unfolding, it took a great effort to keep a sense of urgency from his voice when Papa placed a long-distance phone call to his parents in Vietri. "Mamma, it's Carmine! *Si, va tutto bene*! Call Papa to the phone so you can both listen together, ok?" Waiting barely five seconds, Papa relayed the same to Nonno, that all is well here. We knew long distance calls can be a source for concern, especially for grandparents, so all the pleasantries were exchanged, news from both sides of the ocean was discussed, and familiar love and laughter set everyone at ease.

"Angelina was trying to reach her brother, Fabio, but the brass at his base won't give us information about his whereabouts. We wondered when you had last heard from him?" Papa paused, listening for a few minutes, then placed his hand over the receiver and told us that Fabio was there, in Vietri, but had some friends to catch up with, so he might not be back at Nonni's home for another hour or more.

"Papa and Mamma, we miss you so dearly. I'm glad to hear you've been showing off Julietta's pictures to everyone. She's really quite a good photographer, *no*? Nico has become an excellent researcher, assisted by his sweetheart, Luca. Yes, she is the beautiful blonde girl in the photo. Julietta is very fond of a fine young man, Frank Ernst, and they too are inseparable. He's the one who stands about an inch shorter next to her. We've been fortunate to have become friends with Luca's father and Frank's parents. But I guess Angelina has written you about them." The conversation shifted to my Nonni's end until I heard Papa say, "*Certo!* Angelina is the treasure of my life, like you are to each other!"

Like most overseas calls, this one had static, periods of nothing heard, and the very real likelihood of someone listening in. But every word was lapped up, like a thirsty dog grateful for a bowl of water. And like that dog's experience, love was at the center of each tidbit to be cherished for long after the voices were heard only within one's memory. Papa used his free hand to speak as if his *genitori* were present in our kitchen, although we knew his parents were on another continent. "Mamma, you'd better be taking care of my Papa -- he sounds like he's wasting away! What? He's eating too much? Maybe he should be spending more time writing to us! It takes up to four weeks to get your letters by ship, but we don't care if the news is old, just keep writing!"

"Put me on the phone, Carmine. I miss them so much my hands are trembling with anticipation!" Mamma spoke up, and waited several minutes for Papa to shut up and let her talk. "*I miei piu cari*! she said to her 'dearest ones'. "We are missing you every day and night. How I would love to have a game of rummy and a glass of Nonno's wine with his homemade sausage. Nothing here compares. Carmine's sausage is too lean, and he doesn't grind the fennel seeds like you do. Come and visit us before Nico finishes college and Julietta is engaged!"

At that, Nico and I clamored for our turn, but Mamma wouldn't relinquish the phone, so we snuck behind her and started making animal sounds, which produced howls from the folks on the receiving side. Mamma gave up and handed the phone to Nico, but not before she asked them to be sure to have Fabio call as soon as he returned.

We all exchanged our love and shared our latest escapades. Their elderly neighbor had become feeble and was convinced by her daughter to live with her family in

Salerno. She refused to go until my Nonni promised they would look out after her hens, all spoiled pets to her. And *le polizia* had stopped by the butcher shop advising them to keep a sharp lookout for a non-local swindler who has been defrauding other shopkeepers. Turns out this policeman was a classmate of Nico's. Nonno thanked him with a chub of salami and heard nothing more on that subject. Maybe he was just wanting to show up and say *Ciao*? Love and laughter again and the line went too fuzzy to hear so we hung up and waited for Fabio to call. Barely an hour passed when we received the call.

"Fabio, is that you? What took you so long? I have important news I need your help to digest," Mamma said in one breath. "Monsignor has been truly treacherous, Fabio! He implanted an heirloom necklace with exquisite gems and gold in the globe our Infant of Prague holds. What? You are not surprised? *Si*, this is agonizing to us, and we want your advice and help to end this evil. He put us in peril to assist the Nazis, who he also helped flee to Argentina. We are still in danger, Fabio!" Mamma went on to convey the story, abbreviated but adequate enough to alarm her brother.

"You mean it? You will really try to assist us? Of course, and you can fly here? Nico and I have placed the necklace in a safe deposit box, and Brenda Ernst -- yes, Frank's mother -- volunteered to craft an imposter from photos she took. Fabio, this necklace is exquisite, and I fear it's also an object which will put us in great danger."

Returning the receiver to the wall receptable, she turned to my overeager family and announced we had an ally in the matter. "My brother is flying to Cordoba as soon as he can, and will help us make the best decisions. Who would be more effective than a seasoned spy who knows better than to trust anyone, but leads them to believe he is trusting them?"

Papa and I clapped our hands and Nico said, "I want to be the driver to pick him up. Take me for practice lessons so I can get licensed. Let's get started!" We did, and surprised Fabio three days later when, after the long flight to Buenos Aires, changing planes for Cordoba, he arrived just in time for a late dinner of manicotti, pesto tomato salad, and the best wine Mamma could procure. Typically Italian, we ate, drank, and gestured crazily as we talked and each of us clamored for Tio Fabio's attention.

"Where are those photos of the treasure found in your heirloom Infant? Bring them and the camera here, Julietta." the Captain commanded. Expecting this, I had them ready and we all quieted down, amazingly, while he thumbed through and said, "*Madonna*! This really is a treasure. And it fit inside that tiny globe?" Laughter pealed from him, infecting us as we poured more wine and passed the cuccidati, baked fresh yesterday while we waited for his arrival. "Has your Mrs. Ernst created the decoys yet? I hope she's as good as you report. I was suspicious of her family for a while, but I'll place my suspicions instead onto our actual international criminal conspirator, the good Monsignor. Come on, you agree he was behind this!" Fabio challenged us.

"I've brought more secretly obtained information exposing the complicity of the Genovese Patriarchs, the Vatican, and the revered Peróns. It'll make the hair on your arms rise! It was a very close call and heaven knows -- I say that figuratively -- you were in danger if they'd drawn a gun on you rather than bolting out. Let's strategize in the morning, after I've digested this wonderful meal. *Grazie!* sis and Carmine. I cannot tell you how grateful I am you're all healthy and safe. I'm going to be sure you stay that way!"

Mamma showed him his room, stayed and talked with him past our bedtime, and still she was up to serve breakfast, looking happier than I'd seen her in a long time. "No fair," I protested, as Mamma insisted Nico and I get off to our respective schools and shoved lunch bags in our hands as she rushed us out the door. She added, "Fabio and I are meeting Brenda Ernst at the bank vault and then she will drive us on a tour of Cordoba, stopping at Café los Angelitos for coffee and panini, since Fabio refuses to drink maté. We will catch him up with all the details before we pick you and Frank up from high school, Juli, and then meet Nico back at the house around five. Fabio will be staying with us until we have a few plans formulated and rehearsed, and he promises to fill us in on his exploits and the everyday life of our Vietri family."

THIRTY-TWO

MADONNA OF FALSE HOPE

Fabio fingered through the issue of Life featuring Argentina's first lady, Eva Perón in her illustrious Christian Dior gown, ostentatious jewels bespeaking her impeccable taste and wealth, and the rehearsed smile of the madonna she believed herself to be. Didn't most Argentineans adulate everything about her, placing her just below sainthood? "Much more attractive than Lady Clementine Churchill, right?" he chided. "Her extravagant European tour has been the topic of conversations bringing cheer to citizens all over Europe. Breath-taking was the term the newspapers used regarding her entrance when visiting dignitaries of Spain, France, Germany and Italy as they fawned all over her. Sickening is the term I would apply to "The Lady of Hope".

"Sis, here's the photo of Evita greeted by Generalissimo Franco of Spain, with the utmost spectacle imaginable -- countless uniformed guards, folkloric dancers, 300,000 delirious Spaniards calling out her name, and red carpet stretched out for miles, bordered by flowers of Spanish red-yellow-red, and the Argentinean blue-white-blue flags everywhere. Motorcades, processions, gifts, including a carpet with the reproduction of an El Greco painting! Even holidays were called in her honor. Franco was startled, and in no manner happy, when his extravaganza only produced the promise of one ship load of wheat!" His last comment brought a howl of laughter at the disappointment of the "little general".

"The insanity of it all -- pomp and circumstance and the ungodly addiction to fashion -- she wore her sable cape in the extreme heat of a southern European summer, and she insisted on visiting slums, even entering dilapidated houses while making sure the press heard her talking to disadvantaged residents about social aid and justice, telling them about the generosity of her husband, President Juan Perón. She was even heard to say, on a visit to the palace of King Philip II in Madrid, "So many rooms! We could make a great home for orphans here!"

Mamma couldn't contain herself laughing when she commented, "We were warned the very day of our arrival, by Paolo we had better not belittle the reverence shown to Evita by her people. That's blasphemy!" She then reported to us, "Fabio waited until you arrived here to read on about Evita's tour of Rome and the Vatican." I sat as close as possible to him on the sofa, while Nico and Mamma pulled their chairs closer to view the magazine photos he referred to.

"Ah, *si*! The Vatican debacle, which began by her oversleeping and being late for her audience with Pope Pius XII in the Papal library, wearing a long black dress and off-kilter hairdo. Multiple monsignors greeted her as she strode into the Papal chambers. It has been reported that Eugenio Pacelli, known as Pius XII, spoke of President Perón as 'his favorite son,' a precious rampart against communism. After a generous 20-minute visit, only offered to queens, Evita reported the visit went well and gave a substantial contribution to the Papacy. She was then whisked off to Rome, where we later learned she arranged for the most heinous Croatian war criminal, Ante Pavelic, head of the fascist Ustashi, to receive a visa for Argentina and a passport from the International Red Cross. It was known even then, Pavelic had been responsible for the death of 800,000 people in concentration camps throughout Croatia. *800,000!* Cover your ears if you would be haunted by his words: 'A good Ustashi is he who can use his knife to cut a child from the womb of its mother.' By traveling to Argentina disguised as a Catholic priest, he slipped through the hands of Americans who wanted him to be extradited for his war crimes. Oops! How could that have happened?"

"Don't make me laugh again, Fabio, or I'll spill my coffee," Mamma said, suppressing a giggle. Fabio continued, "Following her successes and foibles throughout the three months of her 'Rainbow Tour' through great halls of Europe, was Otto Skorzeny, the mastermind most responsible for planning and building the escape route for Nazi elite and SS members, called ODESSA. Believing there was a link with the cash she was handling and the Reichsbank gold mine, 'Scarface' Skorzeny befriended Colonel Juan Perón, making himself essential in the Argentinean police. Perón, who had been an admirer of Mussolini and had trained under him, lauded Skorzeny for his daring rescue of *Il Duce* from the alpine fortress supposedly impossible to reach. Skorzeny ran ODESSA and an organization called *Die Spinne*, or the Spider, a kind of political mafia, with impunity. The intention behind all of this was to restore former Nazi party members into positions of power. Its goal: to usher in the Fourth Reich and take over the world!"

Fabio set aside the magazine and took his sister's hands in his, lifted her and led her back to the kitchen, asking, "Have you heard enough? I have some unsavory stories about Nazis in Argentina I can whisper to you." As always, he made her laugh, while she opened a package of figs, almonds and hazelnuts for a quick snack before they headed off to the bank vault.

Mrs. Ernst was waiting for them in the baroquely ornate Banque Credit Suisse. She was in conversation with a bank officer who was quite obviously an admirer, though she would never encourage his attentions. Her smiling eyes opened widely when he greeted her, "*Guten Morgen*, Frau Ernst!"

Mamma reported to us later Brenda was charmed, warmed and immediately cognizant Fabio was extraordinary. And that was before they chatted together at the café, when he responded to her interest in his profession these last ten years. "I wish you could have been there when the box was opened to reveal the real jewels. He listened intently to Brenda describing in detail what they beheld, the estimated market value and replacement values. Most importantly, when Brenda told him this heirloom had a reward associated with its return -- no questions asked -- he nodded gravely and said it can't happen soon enough."

"Which is why I spent fourteen hours creating this duplicate but phony piece. Would you be fooled by the imposter?" she asked, unfolding the fine tissue paper envelope she had placed it in.

Fabio responded, "Goddammit! That is one exceptional work of art, Brenda. Convincing and beautiful enough for Evita herself to proudly grace her slim white neck. I am one fine spy, but I'd take that for authentic. Only when placed next to the real one, is it obvious to be of lesser quality. However, its value for this bait and switch is priceless. Why are you doing this?"

Brenda and Mamma spoke over each other conveying to him how close their mutual interests and friendship has brought them. Their steaming coffees were set down, with a small biscotti alongside the cup, allowing Fabio to relaxedly disclose an abbreviated version of his career, leaving the details and exploits for this evening's dinner with both families at the Ernst's home. "I'm also delaying explaining my two plans. Either plan is plotted to use this carefully crafted sabotage to expose the perpetrators in their complicity, coordinating the movement from Europe of massive ill-gotten wealth and Nazi human predators. You've already played a major role in this, and I hope we can see justice served, despite being unable to extradite the war criminals and slayers of millions themselves."

"After what we have suffered due to the German war machine, yes, a wholehearted yes! Forgive my leave-taking, but I must get the sauerbraten baking so it will fill the house with one of our favorite aromas to greet you at eight tonight. I prepared it in red wine, vinegar, honey, juniper berry and crushed gingersnaps the day Angelina told me they expected you to arrive within the week. Here you are three days later -- impressive, even for a high-ranking captain! The braised red cabbage and apples are already prepared, as their cooking aroma is less pleasant. Angelina is bringing dessert -- heavenly tiramisu, and we'll have coffee in your honor. *Auf wiedersehen!*"

Tio Fabio paid the bill and drove Papa's car to my high school where Frank and I were pacing out front in anticipation. I was giddy about introducing my first love to my treasured uncle, who had commented so beautiful a ring implied as beautiful a love. I could not have agreed more.

"Call me Tio Fabio, Herr Ernst," was his greeting, while extending his hand to Frank, now in the back seat. "I thoroughly enjoyed meeting your talented *Mutti* and can hardly wait to meet your father, and the beloved Luca attached to Nico. We have quite an evening in store for us."

I blurted out, "And quite a week ahead. Hopefully weeks ahead, as I can't bear for you to leave us any sooner."

"Before I leave, I am determined to be able to declare: *'Veni, Vidi, Vici!*"

Frank added, "My Latin is passable, but that is a universal phrase known from Roman Empire days, 'I came, I saw, I conquered!' What will it mean for you to conquer?"

Tio Fabio grinned and said, "You'll find out, starting with dinner tonight." Driving home to meet Nico and Luca and wait for Papa to return from work, we were all talking in turns, even Frank joining in with customary Italian hand gestures and joviality. Mamma mentioned she wanted to bring Fabio to church at the Basilica, itself of cultural significance, well worth a visit. She felt compelled to have him meet Father Russell, especially since she held the cleric at arm's length with suspicion.

Tio Fabio mocked, "May I deliver up a prayer to Our Lady of Perpetual Exhaustion, then? I shall entreat her to save us from unendurable ineptitude and black-cassocked religious who pretend to be following the will of God, while we recognize their actual agenda is to follow the money."

Nobody could express *that* any better, and we laughed without reserve. The laughter ended when Fabio produced the necklace from Mrs. Ernst and asked to be shown how to place it into the orb held by the Infant of Prague. Mamma jumped up and brought it over to him, deftly opening it with her hairpin. "*Scusi*, sis. I'm going to bless this as I place it in and pray no harm comes while the Christ child is looking over you. That's about what Monsignor said when he blessed it and piously handed it to you, *no*?"

While Tio Fabio was making the sign of the cross and blessing the treasure he then placed in the orb, Papa arrived, dashed to wash up and change for dinner and returned to join the fun we were having.

Frank reminded us we should be on our way, so Nico drove us to his house and Dr. Ernst greeted us at the door, beaming at Fabio, with a genuine welcome. He had warmed so to our family since our earliest meetings, and was as welcoming to my uncle. "Have they been filling your head with the intrigues and revolutionary ideas we have been brewing over the recent few weeks? I hope so, because once you're caught up with all of that, we can brainstorm how to catch the perpetrators and maybe even net some Nazis in the same scheme."

As they took seats in the parlor, Fabio took the lead, "Here's how we approach it: the genuine heirloom necklace will be safely stowed in the bank safe deposit box until after the next retrieval attempt is finally foiled. I know how effective the Church network is. Like a spider web it will attract and then capture its victims. Only, its victims are its faithful congregants, so the subterfuge and complicity of which we are now aware will continue to endanger their own."

Papa added, "Sure, while they reap the profitable share of Nazi elite's endowment of the spoils of war and the very real Jewish genocide. Huge quantities of irreplaceable art and treasures, gold and jewels they have hidden away, are to be used like a virgin's dowry to provide for them in a new land."

"The next attempt is imminent, I am certain," inserted Mamma. "I already have suspicions that another of the

Church's unsuspecting faithful will be captured in its web and will attempt to retrieve the jewels. As far as they know, we are not aware of the treasure within our treasure, the Infant of Prague. I find it hideous Jesus should be the magnet attracting the iron-hearted through the Church's schemes. Should I prepare for another deceitful move by a false pawn to befriend me so the Church's quest might be fulfilled? How?"

"Angelina, I hate for you to be the decoy, but since I have been trained so deeply in espionage, I will prepare you to be the unsuspecting lure AND the crafty detective. You must catch the thief or thieves in the act, so set the trap appropriately, to allow the attempt to appear successful. We will then be able to track the movement of the duplicated jewels I suspect will lead directly or indirectly to Monsignor. Oh, how I wish I could stay long enough to be part of the trap, but I am on leave of active duty and my instructions are to return within a week." Fabio then walked over and placed an arm around both Papa and Dr. Ernst who were standing together. "See, I leave you in good hands here. I don't trust just anyone with my only sister's life!"

Nico then urged Tio Fabio to tell us what the other scheme would entail. "Is there a role for me. I vow to protect my Mamma as well!"

"Right on target, my always prepared nephew! Should that trap not succeed, you and others in your group will need to learn to be covert trackers. Oh, I will make good spies of you! We'll succeed in forcing the Church to return to its mission of helping the poor, saving the souls of the wicked, or at least the wayward, being the Good Shepherd to flocks of baptized Catholics and staying the hell out of the wholly illegal Nazi resettlement effort, forever! Are you in?" Fabio turned directly to Nico as he asked.

"Put that way, there's no way you could boot me out. Anyone wishing out, speak up now. Well then silence conveys agreement. I'll affirm the others in our group will also be willing and competent accomplices in your spider's web of intrigue. Let's do it!" Nico emphatically engaged us all in espionage and the pursuit of justice. Of course!

THIRTY-THREE

TAINTED JEWELS

The emaciated, young woman unsteadily entered the basilica, tears still streaming down her hollow cheeks, not even wearing a head covering! It was Saturday noon, so she was certain confession was being held, since tomorrow would be high mass, and all the faithful, desirous to receive communion, must have their souls cleansed by confessing their sins and offering the required penance. Ahead of her was an elderly man, shuffling his way up the long nave to the ornately carved wooden confessionals on each side of the altar. He moved aside, needlessly, as aisles were much wider in a basilica than in a parish church. While she passed him, he glanced at her with scorn. She was thinking her penance would keep her kneeling afterwards for a considerable time and gulped imagining that, noticing her long penance, he would have even more reason for scorn towards her. Once you've confessed and received penance, you would leave the confessional, head bowed and kneel at the altar to offer those obligatory prayers. She knew today's penance would require at least two rosaries, ten Our Father's, twenty-five Hail Mary's, and twenty-five Glory Be's, for she was about to speak the unutterable. Wasn't the greatest sin blaspheming the Lord, our God?

Valeria quietly broke down, saying, "Padre, I have been crying for the last hour. My eyes are red and swollen. My throat is sore from the mucous draining from my running nose. I have a battle between my brain and my soul, creating a raging fury, making me cry out to God, 'why have you done this to me!' Padre, the clinic doctor just confirmed I am with my sixth child!" Valeria burst again into uncontrollable sobs, reaching into her purse for an already overused handkerchief. "I have no energy and no money to care for the five children God has already entrusted me with.

The youngest is only one year old and still nursing! Why, Padre? Why does God make me suffer so?"

"Listen to me, my dear faithful one. God never gives us greater hardships than we can bear! Keep this in mind as I ask you to focus on Blessed Virgin Mary, a mere adolescent who was visited by Archangel Gabriel, when he announced she would be with child. Imagine her shock to learn *this* child would be the long-awaited Savior promised by God to be sacrificed for the redemption of humankind. She was betrothed to blessed Joseph, but she had never been with a man. Gabriel assured her God would bless their union, and our heavenly Father would provide all they would need to raise His only Son! The holy church teaches all life is sacred, for God himself implants a soul at the time of the union which has created new life. You must believe these words, my dear!"

"I will do as you say, Padre, but how can I overcome the revulsion I feel towards my husband for forcing me into the act at a time when I begged him to wait, to avoid conception? How are we going to get by, when he places his desires above the good of the family, leaving us so financially deficient I feel despair? Phillip is a union man, making a decent wage, but his disregard to my pleading for him to drink less so the rest of the family can have adequate food and clothing falls always on deaf ears."

"Valeria, I know your conditions, your family, your voice, and your faith. I know you can do this, but to address the concerns of having adequate provisions, I can offer you greater financial stability, enough to last for some years down the road. As your confessor, I am also a source of God's grace, faithful one. I hear your anguish, far worse than other troubling times when we have previously spoken.

Remember I had asked a favor of you and Phillip. Do you recall?"

"*Si, Padre*. I have befriended Angelina and had meals with her, even at her house, as you requested. It feels so wrong to be suspicious of such a good and generous Catholic woman, Padre! Her family is sweet and most pious - they cannot have Communist leanings. As you know, they have a lovely old-world altar with the Infant of Prague as its centerpiece. Angelina brought me to see the statue dressed in an ornate robe, crossing herself as we approached it. It is sacred to her, Padre, so how can she have ungodly communist leanings? What more can I report?"

"You have done well, and in such a short time, my good and faithful woman! It is because the Vatican itself has formally requested, I found someone like you to assist in recovering what they say are stolen gems, and I have made these requests of you. The Holy Father is infallible, and his dictates from the Vatican are handed down to the faithful to accomplish the most sacred deeds in furtherance of the faith. Look back, Valeria, at the unwavering assistance the Church has provided hiding our Jewish and Italian brethren from Nazi S.S., who would stop at nothing to round them up, force them into railroad cars and send them to labor camps. We hid these Italians, many of whom were Jewish, in convents and amongst the faithful who do not despise Jews. The Vatican has engaged the assistance of many nations to bring these and any Catholics who were likely to become Nazi prisoners, or worse, to the Americas. We would never do this for atheistic communists, and we do not do this for political leftist radicals who would overthrow legitimate governments."

"But, Padre, what does this have to do with me? What are the stolen gems of which you speak? I found nothing about Mrs. Migliore to be suspicious, but I must know more about the mission in which you want me to play a role. In my state of miserable chaos, I need to have my task spelled out for me."

"Valeria," spoke Padre Russell more gently, but still with conviction and urgency, "the Vatican clerics told me specifically the stolen gems are in the possession of the Migliore's and are to be found in the orb of the Infant of Prague statue."

Valeria let out an audible gasp, "Oh no! How can they be certain of this? Must I steal the statue from their house and bring it to you?"

"My dear, there is a hinged release at the rear base of the band encircling the orb. You need only depress the hidden mechanism by pushing a hairpin into it. That will release and open the hinge, revealing a silk sack with a jeweled necklace, given to Vatican clerics to provide support for the endangered political and religious whom we have helped to safety in Argentina. I explained already it is our duty to assist these people, but we do not ask the Catholic faithful to pay for them. That is the purpose for which gems and gold are smuggled here and it is urgent we retrieve them so these downtrodden can begin a new life. You will benefit, as the Church will pay you well for doing its work, for being a tool of the will of God."

Father Russell added, "There is no time to waste. We need to send our next cache of retrieved gems, art and gold to be exchanged for cash to assist those in need and your family. Tell me when you will do this, and I will consider that a significant portion of your penance. You must still pray five Our Father's and ten Hail Mary's. Then, compose yourself and allow God's grace to carry the joy of this new life to your family. God makes no mistakes, my dear Valeria!"

After an extended pause, although still sobbing, Valeria spoke to Father Russell.

"Phillip is sober enough on Saturdays to take the children out for an excursion. I will comply with all the Church asks of me. How much money will be rewarded to us? I have too little to pay the rent and heat as of now, and I'll need more food, especially in my condition." Valeria's voice conveyed a shaky commitment, but it was enough for Father Russell to consider this confession concluded. He promised she would be provided an adequate allowance for an entire year and he'd pray for Phillip to reduce the alcohol consumption and get a higher paying position at the meat packing plant. In fact, he assured her he could make that happen.

Angelina suggested she could deliver the packet of clothes and shoes she had collected for my children, but I lied and told her I would be seeing a dentist in her neighborhood and would enjoy sharing a maté together again. Her door was open on this beautiful afternoon, so I stepped onto the threshold and called to her. She walked over to me with a bushel of laundry she was planning to hang on the clothesline out back. I motioned to take them from her, and she waved me aside, "I have reserves of strength and a few pounds I'd be happy to shed, but come out back with me and hand me the clothespins, would you please?"

While we worked together, she asked me about the children and myself. "I noticed you look more pale than last time I saw you, so I'm concerned since you seem unhealthily thin. What is going on with you, Valeria?" she probed with more than casual concern.

"Why not grab the thermos on the kitchen table and a gourd. The yerba maté and sugar are on the table so pour what you like, sit down and relax. I'll join you when I have the rest of this hung."

"I'm uncommonly tired all the time, and have not been eating well. Plus, there's been nausea. One or more of the kids is down with something every week. Phillip was down with a miserable head cold and out of work for much of last week." I dodged the urgency to tell her about my pregnancy.

Taking her advice, I strolled into the kitchen and fixed my maté, then went towards the altar in the living room. Another round of nausea nearly made me drop my gourd of hot liquid, so I steadied myself, set it down and removed a pin from my hair. Lina had most of the basket left to hang, and some dried towels to fold and bring in, so I was certain she would be nearly ten minutes before joining me. I took this "opportunity" and took my chances. My hands trembled more with detesting myself and my insecure nature than out of fear, but I should have been afraid. Just as Padre said, it was easy to push the end of my hairpin into the visually undetectable spot. It was easy to open the orb and remove the necklace. It was easy to slip it into my pocket. But the hinge resisted closing, despite my most careful efforts. On the fourth attempt, I heard the tiny snap which ultimately closed the orb, only to find Lina peering at me as she entered the room.

"I...I'm attracted to your altar," I stammered. She was about to speak when I blurted out, "I'm pregnant and very upset. Would you please pray with me? I don't think I can even stand on my feet another minute!"

"Valeria, you tried to hide your pregnancy from me, but why? I care about you and your condition, but now I feel a lack of trust you were not going to confide in me. And what is going on with my statue?"

I was so exposed, caught nearly in the act, I ran to the bathroom and vomited. Lina rushed to me and held me up as I nearly collapsed. She looked alarmed as she put her arms underneath mine and helped me to the sofa to lie down. "You rest now. Say nothing until you have regained your strength and then I want to have a heart-to-heart. Do you know what I mean?" I nodded, closed my eyes, and prayed she wouldn't ask again about the statue. Several minutes later, Lina pulled a chair towards the sofa so she could comfort me with water and a biscuit, but she offered no hug. She was angry, but waited until I had regained my composure.

"If you have more to tell me, come out with it now. Don't hold back -- it will only make you weaker and ruin our friendship if you do. Nico will be back from classes in twenty minutes, and I'll have him accompany you home. Know this, Valeria ... I detect deception, and while I sympathize with your pregnancy, I am intolerant of lying. Out with it!"

"There's nothing to tell, Lina. I'm only confused and sick, and I wouldn't lie to a friend. I want to be friends! Phillip and Padre Russell are the only persons who know about my condition, so before I could even tell my parents, I hadn't the strength to tell you," I wailed.

Lina picked up the statue, fingered the orb, and with a slight shake called out to me, "Liar! Admit you were sent to retrieve something of value! It must have been Padre Russell who put you up to this and I expect an answer, as well as for you to return the item you stole."

"But I was given a mission to retrieve a valuable taken by the Nazis to ...

My God, I may faint again. I don't know what I'm talking about. I'm going home!" I tried to rush past her, but she stopped me firmly. "You may go home after you return the stolen piece," she insisted. I broke free by stamping on her foot and running out the still open door, to the bus stop down the block and onto the bus as it was closing its doors. It wasn't even the right bus, but I would not give her back the jewels. They weren't hers anyway! I'd return them to Padre who would use them in the service of God.

Where I got the strength to make it home, I don't know. I collapsed the moment I closed our door and told Andrew not to let anyone in.

If you cannot trust your priest and confessor, who can you trust, I reminded myself. As I fingered the necklace in my pocket, I asked myself again, who is there to trust?

Hours later, Andrew woke me and said Padre Russell was at the door. I responded, "Let him in, and watch the children while the Padre and I have a few minutes."

THIRTY-FOUR

WHEN TRUTH IS TOLD

Valeria: Deed done, necklace handed over to Padre, payment to me of $400 with monthly benefits of $150 to continue. I can trust the Padre, so I feel relieved. Lina's collection of clothes and shoes for my children fit so nicely, but I won't be requesting anything more from her, not even maternity clothes. She must be plenty upset with me. Still, I trust Padre. Everything will be alright. Maybe a little more sleep after I hide the money from Phillip. Maybe if I don't eat enough the baby will not grow inside me. Maybe I can lose the baby, the ability to conceive and the hatred I feel towards myself for betraying Lina. But I trust Padre. Yes, he is providing for me and the faithful.

Angelina: Maybe I will live in conditions conducive to kindness and trust again. I have suffered betrayals and I have gloried in my new friendships. My mamma always told me to count my blessings, which I would do with her nearly every night as we prayed together. The deep grief over losing her will never die. It has barely faded, as I permit myself to move forward in life. My children will never know their lost loved ones, but maybe we will be connected again with our loved ones still in Vietri. Maybe I don't have to look over my shoulder at every step, every action, every communication. I probably always will, with all the courage I can muster. Carmine and Fabio tell me to look around every corner, but I am equally influenced by Nico who, in the name of justice, will throw caution to the wind. Surrounded by Nazis, devious clergy, growing tyranny, oppression and subterfuge, will I feel safe again? Probably not.

Brenda Ernst: These intrigues both sicken and excite me. I am both a player and an observer, both a friend to Angelina and a mentor and friend to Julietta. I am fielding thrusts, and also parrying them; My husband and my son are both becoming more independent of me, but I have yet to re-establish my own independence and identity. I'm as conflicted as my birth country. On one side is fascism and its propaganda, tyranny and murderous legacy; on the other side is my democratic idealism and the determination to resist authoritarianism. I'm not torn asunder, just sort of cracked. Like the lens on Julietta's view finder. Cracked, emotionally as I question whether I am fulfilling my purpose.

Carmine: *Nel bene e nel male*, neither good nor bad. Just consequences. *Nel bene e nel male*. Work, church, thoughts, healing. Just as concerning as frighteningly real. I participate, I support, I parent, I love. I anger easily, I warm slowly. I am someone's son, someone's husband, brother to some, father to some, uncle to many. Yet, I question what my existence is except in those relationships. Thefts target me: against my body and my mind; against my possessions and my decency. But I show up. I steal from no one.

With deep understanding from what I have learned in my forty-two years, I must act. I still have the heart and reasoning of a resistance fighter! I just need to buck up my determination with prowess. It's not my body now, but my experience that is needed on front lines battling for freedom and truth. Yet another resistance against another despotic regime!

Angelina is at my side; Nico and Julietta are positive influencers and wondrous individuals. My adored Papa and Mamma value me and my family and have imparted the greatest depths of their love and wisdom to us. There is no reason to question if I have wisdom enough for the confidence to act, to show up for justice, to love without bounds, and to be a support for them. My God, we are playing a role right now in the destiny of a free world.

Salvatore: I am witness to the sweeping epidemic of disillusionment. Papa could not reconcile remaining in his own homeland; Mamma has been befriended by a priest and at least two women whose motives were to use her, flatter her, trick her, betray her, and possibly kill her. Luca and Julietta are so innocent, so smart, so unique and so trusting, but like me, they are swept into this maelstrom and political clouds, all are ominous, leaving our futures darkening and leaving us engulfed in disillusionment. I am witness to the certainties of war and the uncertainties of peace. I am preparing for a future of powerful actions. At my heart is the need for compassion, at my gut is the need for justice, at my brain is the need for knowledge, and at my soul is the need for respect earned by those who administer the law fairly. I can use the law to erase disillusionment. The loving advice from my Nonno at our final dinner will burn eternally in my life as I use the strength of my Nonno and my Papa to adhere to principles of genuine justice.

Paolo: Always I have been the stalwart, but never, never the bully. My family, my supervisors and my workers look to me for the most efficient direction and correct analyses. I think on my feet and then I act. Look to me for handling your needs, but never, never ask me to be your master. Look to me for strength, resources, skills, and leadership, but don't expect of me to be patient or understanding. Unless you truly are a child, then I expect you to grow up and don't look to me to do it for you. But look to me for protection. I can promise you I will stop at nothing to protect my loved ones.

Raymond: For all my education, honors and achievements, my self-esteem feels like a pretense. I rely on Brenda for everything outside of my surgical practice. I rely on Frank for his brightness and positive outlook on life and the future. I rely on everything to be set in motion for me, after which I will walk the path shown to me. I rely on books, music, a stoic countenance, a practiced composure. Since the horrors of the complete degradation of my countrymen and fatherland, I have lost faith. I look through the windows of life before Krystallnacht, and I see the possibility of joy, and possibility of terror. Oh, God! Do I have to keep making choices?

Frank: Be honest, even if it scares you. I will be honest; I can't hide behind pretenses, so I never scare. Deluding others is so unnatural, of that I am incapable. When I review the plights of my family, my sweet Julietta's family, our closest friends and students in the underground revolutionary movement, I may feel their vulnerability and pain, but I am astonished it doesn't reach into my spirit. Honesty through rose colored glasses? Bifocal vision through the view which I use to focus on life? I attribute my invulnerability and ease while walking through life as courage. I do not harbor fear.

Luca: I have steeped myself in the lives, history, politics and personages of the too recent war and Hitler's extermination camps which killed 13 million innocent Jews, Poles, Russians, Slavs, Romas, academics, doctors, physical and mental misfits, and Africans. Anyone suspected of subversion or disloyalty to Hitler, could expect swift execution would be their fate! I want to scream! The pains inflicted on my father and me at every turn in the road have damaged us. Poland was attacked both from Germans and Soviets, conquered and occupied. Millions of Poles were killed, captured, starved, and forced to labor in factories making armaments that would kill their countrymen. In Poland, my countrymen would not collaborate with the Germans. Yet in Poland nine concentration camps were found. Our government passed anti-Semitism laws! The Warsaw ghetto, and the uprising there was too horrific to describe, and the bombings which killed my mama will always haunt me and will prescribe my journalism. My smile is beautiful, they say. Nico loves equally the fire inside me. Nobody recognizes what I can't even mention, that I truly want to scream!

Walter: Forgiveness is the Way. Forgiving your enemies; forgiving your loved ones; forgiving your country. These I am learning to do. Forgiving myself, I haven't the strength or beliefs I'll need to do this. Such a sorry man. A successful merchant, printer, father, community member, but a failure. For I cannot forgive myself that I allowed my wife to go out on a mission of mercy to the Jewish community being persecuted, and Jews being hidden. She was blown to bits by explosives surrounding the Warsaw

Ghetto, meant to keep Jews in and possible saboteurs out. She was blown to bits, leaving my heart and soul in similar shambles forever. I cannot forgive myself. Even the Lord cannot forgive my negligence. Precious Luca has forgiven me, but I fear she's living with a crater where once was the central part of her heart, my wife. I don't want to forget my dreams. I don't care to remember places and people in my past, but I cannot lose my dreams. I will have them!

Julietta: I'm a traveler. I've traversed the roads from Italy to Argentina, on a journey from Fascism to Populism. New life, different Fascism. I've been moved witnessing widespread despoilment of war, persecution by tyrants and now another repressive government. Moved to activism and to love for humanity. Moved to be a lifelong learner. Moved to be a powerfully insightful photojournalist. Moved to speak and show the truth. Moved to carry on the legacy of my beautiful Italian heritage. At the most stable center of me -- my core -- I have been moved. I'll carry my pains, loves and history with me as I record my journey. My career will enable me to focus on people and events of significance through my life, so I can be a force for others to be moved. I am certain of the strength, fostered in me by *mi genitori*, who have provided the driving force for others to see the truth and never forget. I'll place evidence of critical truths in front of everyone to assure they will never forget!

THIRTY-FIVE

TWO MESSAGES

F ather Russell dawdled as he left the Western Union telegraph office near San Martin Square. It was a beautiful day, and it was exhilarating to be passing through the oldest part of Cordoba with its Mission, its popular public plaza and its monument to the liberator of Argentina. People smiled and some, probably his parishioners, waved. The successful completion of his enormous task would certainly bring notice to the hierarchy of clerics assigned to the Basilica. He knew the Genovese bishops and other clerical potentates would pass along knowledge of his successful feat to the Vatican. Glory be to the Father, and to the Son, and to the Holy Ghost, as it was in the beginning, is now, and ever shall be, world without end. Amen. Oh, he felt like singing aloud to the heavens, to the Savior and His Blessed Mother! He passed shops and mercantiles full of items which some few of the immigrants and most of his other parishioners could afford, and he smiled, for his vow of poverty meant he would have no need for materialistic pursuits. Maybe a cigar if it could be obtained, and there was always wine available at the rectory.

He kept a copy of the telegram he just sent, neatly folded, of course.

TO MONSIGNOR OLIVERIO IN VIETRI SUL MARE, PROVINCE OF SALERNO, ITALY:

ASSIGNMENT COMPLETED STOP MISSION SUCCESSFUL STOP COURIER DISPATCHED WITH YOUR QUARRY STOP FUNDS NEEDED TO CONTINUE TO SUPPORT TARGETED PARTICIPANTS STOP THE CHURCH IS THE TOOL OF OUR ALMIGHTY FATHER STOP

That same month, sent from a Western Union telegraph office in Milan:

TO: MONSIGNOR OLIVERIO, IN VIETRI SUL MARE, PROVINCE OF SALERNO, ITALY

ABANDON THE ESCAPE ROUTE STOP LIKE JUDAS ISCARIOT YOU HAVE BETRAYED THE FAITHFUL STOP LIKE PONTIUS PILATE YOU WILL TRY TO WASH YOUR HANDS OF THIS NAZI SUPPORT AND LIKE DANTE ALIGHIERI YOU WILL DESCEND THROUGH A DEEP VALLEY WITH A RIVER OF BOILING BLOOD STOP THAT IS THE STAIN OF YOUR GUILT STOP I WILL SET IN MOTION YOUR DEMISE STOP THE BENEVOLENCE OF THE GENOVESE HIERARCHY IS A SHAM STOP YOU ARE BEING WATCHED SO TAKE NO STEPS TO IMPERIL THE MIGLIORE FAMILY OR I WILL SEE YOU IN HELL STOP

Fabio M. Millitello, Captain, Italian Special Forces

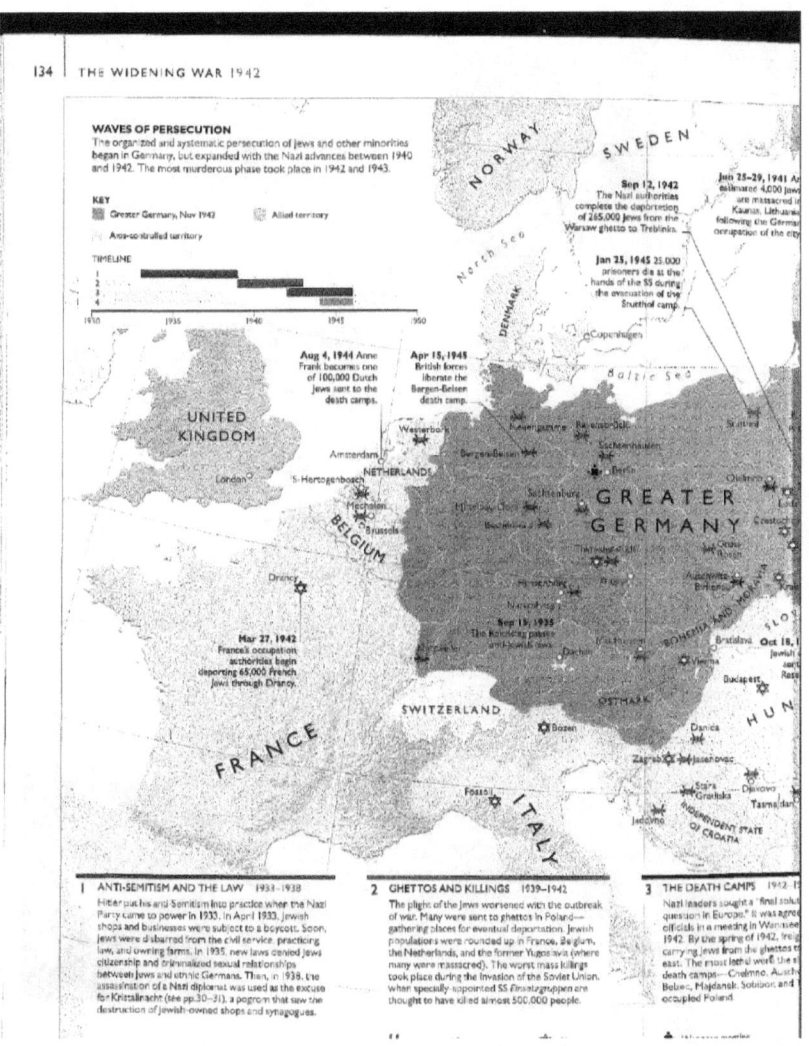

134 | THE WIDENING WAR 1942

WAVES OF PERSECUTION

The organized and systematic persecution of Jews and other minorities began in Germany, but expanded with the Nazi advances between 1940 and 1942. The most murderous phase took place in 1942 and 1943.

KEY

Greater Germany, Nov 1942   Allied territory

Axis-controlled territory

TIMELINE

1930   1935   1940   1945   1950

Sep 12, 1942 The Nazi authorities complete the deportation of 265,000 Jews from the Warsaw ghetto to Treblinka.

Jun 25–29, 1941 An estimated 4,000 Jews are massacred in Kaunas, Lithuania, following the German occupation of the city.

Jan 25, 1945 25,000 prisoners die at the hands of the SS during the evacuation of the Stutthof camp.

Copenhagen

Aug 4, 1944 Anne Frank becomes one of 100,000 Dutch Jews sent to the death camps.

Apr 15, 1945 British forces liberate the Bergen-Belsen death camp.

NORWAY   SWEDEN

North Sea

DENMARK

Baltic Sea

UNITED KINGDOM

London

Westerbork

Amsterdam

NETHERLANDS

's-Hertogenbosch

Mechelen

Brussels

BELGIUM

Drancy

Mar 27, 1942 French occupation authorities begin deporting 65,000 French Jews through Drancy.

FRANCE

SWITZERLAND

Bergen-Belsen   Ravensbrück   Sachsenhausen

Berlin

GREATER GERMANY

Buchenwald

Sep 15, 1935 The Nuremberg passes anti-Jewish laws

Dachau

OSTMARK

Bozen

Vienna

Budapest

HUN

SLO

Bratislava **Oct 18,** Jewish

Auschwitz-Birkenau

BOHEMIA AND MORAVIA

Chelmno

Danica

Zagreb   Jasenovac

Stara Gradiska   Djakovo

Foggia

ITALY

INDEPENDENT STATE OF CROATIA

Jasenovac   Tasmajdan

1 ANTI-SEMITISM AND THE LAW 1933–1938

Hitler put his anti-Semitism into practice when the Nazi Party came to power in 1933. In April 1933, Jewish shops and businesses were subject to a boycott. Soon, Jews were disbarred from the civil service, practicing law, and owning farms. In 1935, new laws denied Jews citizenship and criminalized sexual relationships between Jews and ethnic Germans. Then, in 1938, the assassination of a Nazi diplomat was used as the excuse for Kristallnacht (see pp.30–31), a pogrom that saw the destruction of Jewish-owned shops and synagogues.

2 GHETTOS AND KILLINGS 1939–1942

The plight of the Jews worsened with the outbreak of war. Many were sent to ghettos in Poland—gathering places for eventual deportation. Jewish populations were rounded up in France, Belgium, the Netherlands, and the former Yugoslavia (where many were massacred). The worst mass killings took place during the invasion of the Soviet Union, when specially-supported SS Einsatzgruppen are thought to have killed almost 500,000 people.

3 THE DEATH CAMPS 1942–1

Nazi leaders sought a "final solution" to the Jewish question in Europe." It was agreed by officials in a meeting in Wannsee in 1942. By the spring of 1942, trains carrying Jews from the ghettos to the east. The most lethal were the death camps—Chelmno, Auschwitz, Belzec, Majdanek, Sobibor and Tall in occupied Poland.

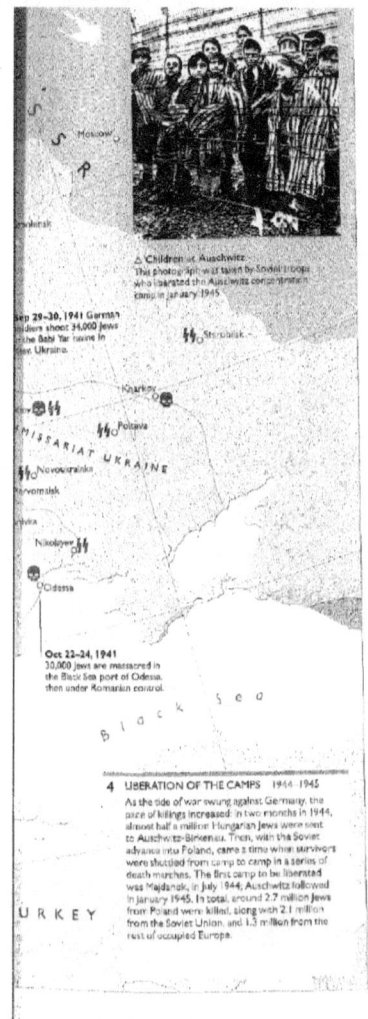

△ Children at Auschwitz
This photograph was taken by Soviet troops who liberated the Auschwitz concentration camp in January 1945

Sep 29–30, 1941 German soldiers shoot 34,000 Jews in the Babi Yar ravine in Kiev, Ukraine.

Oct 22–24, 1941 30,000 Jews are massacred in the Black Sea port of Odessa, then under Romanian control.

4 LIBERATION OF THE CAMPS 1944–1945
As the tide of war swung against Germany, the pace of killings increased: in two months in 1944, almost half a million Hungarian Jews were sent to Auschwitz-Birkenau. Then, with the Soviet advance into Poland, came a time when survivors were shuttled from camp to camp in a series of death marches. The first camp to be liberated was Majdanek, in July 1944; Auschwitz followed in January 1945. In total, around 2.7 million Jews from Poland were killed, along with 2.1 million from the Soviet Union, and 1.3 million from the rest of occupied Europe.

THE
HOLOCAUST

Hitler and his supporters saw the Jews as a worldwide enemy conspiring to undermine the German nation. The Nazi regime embarked on what became known as the Holocaust—the systematic persecution and murder of around six million European Jews.

The Nazi rise to power had immediate consequences for Germany's Jews, who were treated from the start as racial outcasts. From 1935 onward they were denied citizenship and forbidden to marry or have sexual relations with people of "German blood." The policy was deliberately aimed at encouraging Jews to flee the country, and by 1938 about half the Jewish population had done just that.

With the outbreak of war, the situation deteriorated further. Ghettos were created in the occupied eastern lands where deportees could be resettled and controlled. During the drive eastward many Jewish populations were massacred, often in retaliation for isolated acts of resistance. From late 1941, new extermination centers were constructed—known as Operation Reinhard camps—where Jews were sent to the gas chambers or selected for grueling slave labor, through which thousands more were worked to death. The results were horrifying: when liberation finally came, an estimated two-thirds of Europe's pre-war Jewish population had been wiped out.

"The Holocaust was not only a Jewish tragedy, but also a human tragedy."

SIMON WIESENTHAL, HOLOCAUST SURVIVOR

OTHER PERSECUTED MINORITIES

Jews were not the only minority group persecuted by the Nazis. Their victims stretched from homosexual men and people with disabilities to Jehovah's Witnesses, Freemasons, and Catholic and Protestant dissidents. In terms of numbers, ethnic groups suffered the worst losses: Romani people faced the same genocidal threat as the Jews, while the Nazi assault on the Slavic peoples ended in the deaths of some 15 million Soviets and 3 million Poles.

Roma and Sinti women at Bergen-Belsen

www.ingramcontent.com/pod-product-compliance
Lightning Source LLC
Chambersburg PA
CBHW021216130626
46554CB00004B/1248